Gettysburg 1863

High tide of the Confederacy

Campaign • 52

Gettysburg 1863

High tide of the Confederacy

Carl Smith • Illustrated by Adam Hook

First published in Great Britain in 1998 by Osprey Publishing,
Midland House, West Way, Botley, Oxford OX2 0PH, UK
44-02 23rd St, Suite 219, Long Island City, NY 11101, USA
Email: info@ospreypublishing.com

09 10 11 12 13 21 20 19 18 17 16 15 14 13 12

CIP Data for this publication is available from the British Library

ISBN 978 1 85532 336 0

Series Editor: LEE JOHNSON

Editor: Iain MacGregor
Design: The Black Spot

Colour bird's eye view illustrations by Peter Harper
Cartography by Micromap
Battlescene artwork by Adam Hook
Filmset in Singapore by Pica Ltd.
Printed in China through World Print Ltd.

KEY TO MILITARY SERIES SYMBOLS

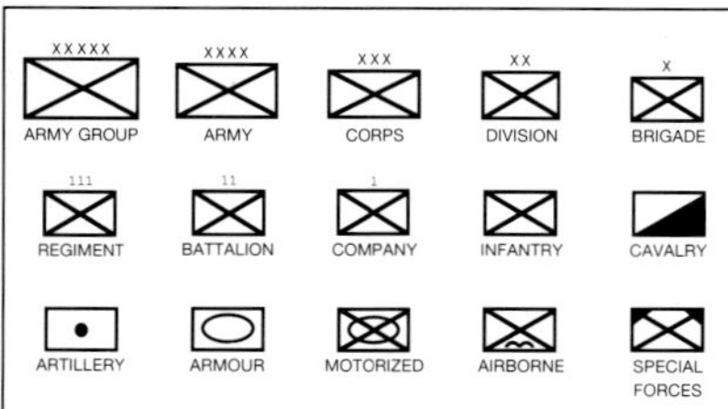

Author's note

Many thanks to the following: West Point Military Museum, Peter Harrington at Anne S K Brown, Scott Hartwig at Gettysburg, and Bill Gallop for their help with the photographs and manuscript.

A guide to further reading

Albright, Harry, *Gettysburg: Crisis of Command*, Hippocrene Books (New York 1983)
Bishop, Chirs, Ian Drury and Tony Gibbons, *1400 Days: The Civil War Day by Day*, Gallery Books (New York 1990)
Catton, Bruce, *The Army of the Potomac: Glory Road*, Doubleday & Company (1952)
Gallagher, Gary W. (Ed), *The Third Day at Gettysburg and Beyond*, University of North Carolina Press (1944)
Hassler, Warren W. Jnr, *Crisis at the Crossroads: The First Day at Gettysburg*, University of Alabama Press (1970)
Long, E.B., and Barbara Long, *The Civil War Day by Day: an Almanac 1861-1865*, Doubleday & Company (1971)
Nesbitt, Mark, *35 Days to Gettysburg: The Campaign Diaries of Two Enemies*, Stockpole Books (1992)
Pfanz, Harry W., *Gettysburg: The Second Day*, University of North Carolina Press (1987)
Raus, Edmund J. Jr, *A Generation on the March – The Union Army at Gettysburg*, H.E. Howard (1987)
Sifakis, Stewart, *Compendium of Confederate Armies: North Carolina*, Facts On File INC, (1992)
Tuker, Glenn, *Lee and Longstreet at Gettysburg*, The Bobbs Merrill Company (1968)
Wheeler, Richard, *Witness to Gettysburg*, Harper & Row Publishers, (1987)

Editor's Note

All photographic material for this book has been supplied by the Anne S. K. Brown Military Collection, Brown University Library.

Artist's Note

Readers may care to note the original paintings from which the colour plates in this book were prepared are available for private sale. All reproduction copyright whatsoever is retained by the Publishers. Enquiries should be addressed to:

Scorpio Gallery, P.O. Box 475, Hailsham, E. Sussex BN27 2SL

The Publishers regret that they can enter into no correspondence upon this matter.

COVER: 'The Battle of Gettysburg: Pickett's Charge' by Peter F. Rothermel. (The State Museum of Pennsylvania)

CONTENTS

MOVES TOWARDS GETTYSBURG, 4 JUNE – 1 JULY, 1863

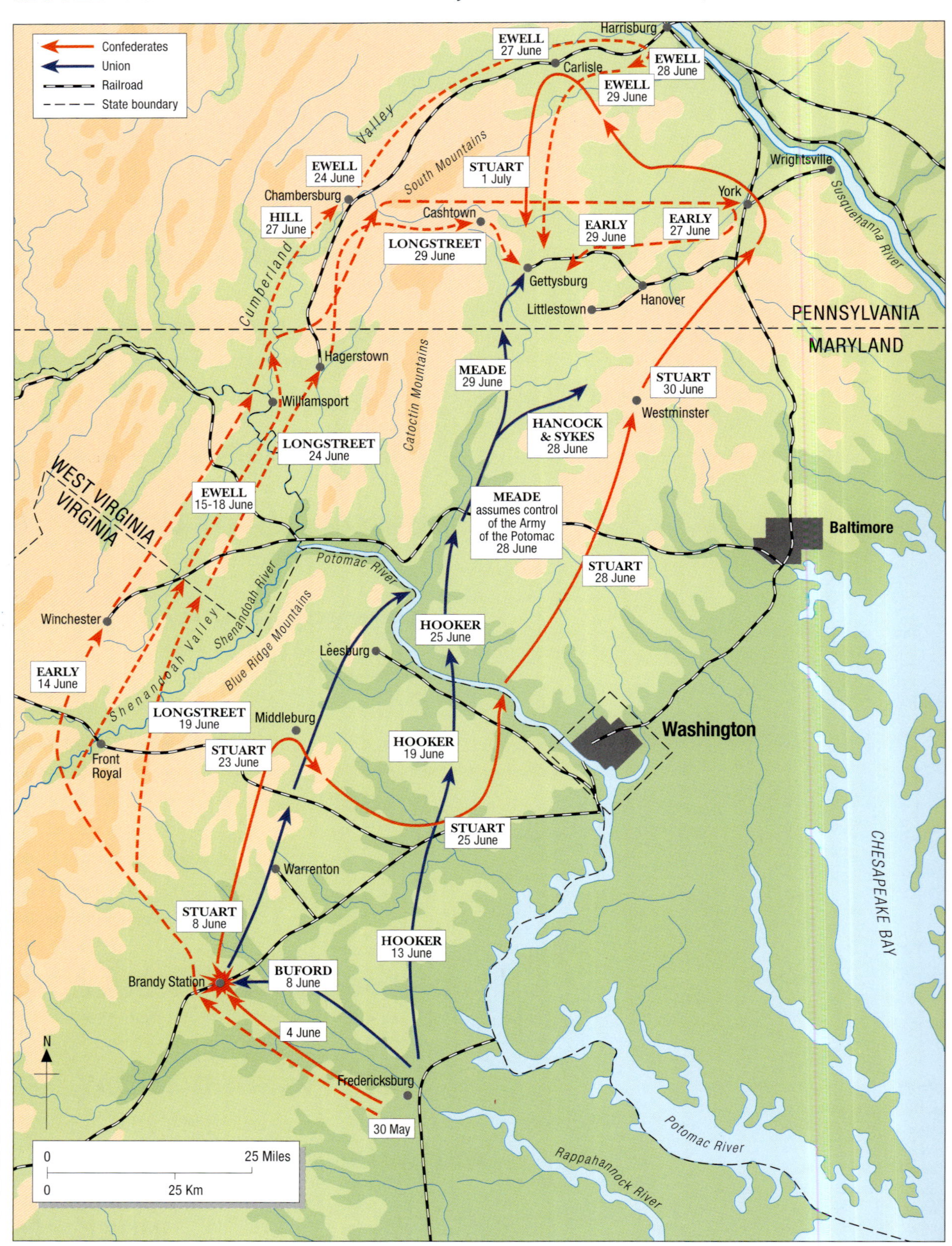

ORIGINS OF THE CAMPAIGN

Gettysburg just seemed to happen. No great plan declared that Meade would stop Lee's army at this spot. The armies, which had been moving on parallel courses, just seemed to blunder into each other and skirmish, and then their respective commanders decided that here was as good a place as anywhere to fight a battle.

Gettysburg was the turning point of the American Civil War: afterwards Confederate hopes of establishing a separate nation dwindled as the likelihood of winning or of enticing European intervention waned. The South did not feel Gettysburg was a pivotal encounter, and Northern voices severely criticized Meade for allowing the Army of Northern Virginia to escape intact. That Gettysburg should occur was inevitable, but that it occurred the way it did – and where it did – was the result of a series of coincidences.

Gettysburg was a city of little military importance. Most of the surrounding area was farmland and orchards, long shorn of old forest growth, and the basically flat lands were broken only by low ridges and gentle hills. Boasting a rail line to the east and an unimproved cut where the track would be laid to the west, the town had a Lutheran seminary on a nearby hill and was the nexus of roads leading to Washington, Philadelphia, or Harrisburg. The steeple of the Lutheran church was the highest man-made site. The rumour of a warehouse filled with shoes may have been started by Heth to justify his contravening Lee's orders not to initiate a general engagement without orders. Until 30 June, there was

Postcard view of Gettysburg's Lutheran Seminary's east side, showing the cupola where Buford watched the Confederate advance. This part reached above the canopy of trees and afforded a clear view of Herr and McPherson Ridges.

Burnside and his staff before Hooker relieved him of command of the Army of the Potomac. Hooker's days were numbered because of his reluctance to engage Lee.

nothing in the area to interest the Union Army – except the Army of Northern Virginia, which had slipped away from Hooker in Virginia and had moved north.

After Fredericksburg and Chancellorsville the Army of the Potomac was demoralized. Their overly cautious fourth commander, Gen. Joseph (Fightin' Joe) Hooker, was wary of being too aggressive after Jackson and Lee's triumph at Chancellorsville, lest Lee leave his fortifications at Fredericksburg, defeat Hooker and then march on to Washington, D.C. with no Union Army to impede him. The spectre of a Confederate advance east burdened every Army of the Potomac commander, but none more so than Hooker.

Events at Gettysburg were set in motion before Fredericksburg. After Antietam, Lee's 1862 northern campaign halted. Yet Lee's desire to invade the Union remained strong, as did his belief that if he could just take the war north, Yankee pro-war sentiments would wane.

Lee had to take the war north. Another summer campaign would be disastrous for Virginia farmers because they could neither plant nor harvest crops. Furthermore, a timely Confederate thrust might relieve pressure on Vicksburg in the west, since Northerners, feeling endangered, might demand placement of military garrisons in their key cities, which would involve withdrawing troops from the west as well as from the east. Finally, if England and France saw an aggressive and victorious Southern Army, either might enter the war on behalf of the beleaguered Confederacy, or at least give the Union good reason to sue for peace with Richmond on its own terms before they took an active interest in the war.

Next to Lee, Jackson had been the most aggressive commander of the South. Jackson's death had removed one half of Lee's corps commanders

LEFT **Maine infantry in 1863 wearing shorter uniform blouses instead of the earlier issue frock coat; the officer wears a shell jacket. Note the variations between officer, drummer, and enlisted field dress. Wearing leggings seemed a matter of individual preference rather than regulation.**

and Lee had had to restaff his command. (Longstreet was good, but cautious.) Time was a constraint: the war had to go north that year, before summer too, otherwise winter would catch the Confederates trying to live off hostile land. Lee well understood the horrors of Napoleon's Moscow campaign, and that his own invasion called for stealth. By quietly moving his army piecemeal, new corps commanders would have time to become acquainted with their responsibilities, with Lee's command style and with the enemy commanders facing them. By the time they engaged in

BELOW **European idealized representations of Confederate and Federal Army uniforms. Although these were the official uniforms, men in the field wasted little time modifying them for battlefield conditions. Many soldiers started out with these uniforms, but by 1863 battlefield dress was for comfort and flexibility; superfluous items had been discarded long ago. Shortage of material, uncertain supply, and field conditions dictated personal uniform modification.**

combat, they would be comfortable with the command structure. Although his corps commanders were new, they were competent generals, and Lee had the greatest confidence in his troops.

Lee's plan was to steal a march on the Army of the Potomac. Once distanced from Federal troops, the Army of Northern Virginia would effectively disappear as Stuart's cavalry screened its movements from Union forces. The Army of Northern Virginia could then strike at Pennsylvania or possibly as far as Harrisburg before swinging down to Maryland, while Stuart's cavalry protected their route of march and denied Hooker intelligence of their actions until it was too late. The Union Army would have to leave Virginia to chase and engage Lee – in a battle at a time and place of Lee's choosing. In so doing he would defeat the Federal Army. He had considered all these factors before Chancellorsville.

CHRONOLOGY

2–4 May – After defeating the Union Army at Chancellorsville, Stonewall Jackson is wounded by his own pickets. Hooker retreats the Army of the Potomac east and north, crossing the Rappahannock, and feels safe once across the river.

10 May – Stonewall Jackson dies from pneumonia, a complication which set in after the amputation of his wounded arm.

30 May – The Army of Northern Virginia (formerly only two large corps) is reorganized into three corps plus Stuart's cavalry division. These are commanded by Lt.Gen. Richard Ewell (est. 20,866 men), Lt.Gen. Ambrose P. Hill (est. 26,793 men), and Lt.Gen. James Longstreet (est. 21,031 men) – Lee's "old warhorse." Of these, only Longstreet is comfortable with Lee's command style and has had experience as a corps commander. Ewell is experienced and has served under Jackson, losing a leg at Second Manassas. Lee thought highly of Hill, although Hill was impatient when it came to waiting for orders through the chain of command and was guilty of having attacked without orders on more than one occasion. Lee may have thought Hill would prove to be as aggressive as Jackson.

3 June – Lee's northern campaign begins when he moves 7,138 troops westward under McLaws of Longstreet's command.

4 June – Lee sends Ewell north after Longstreet, leaving Hill at Fredericksburg to hold Hooker in place by deception (having men tend multiple fires to make it appear that more Confederates are in camp than there realy are). Hooker's cavalry patrols report troop movements, but he is uncertain if these are real troop movements or a relocation of base camps. He senses Lee is setting a trap for him.

5 June – Hooker's scouts report Confederates still dug in at Fredericksburg, although some troop movements have been indicated. Lee's deception is working. Hooker telegraphs Washington: "This morning, some more of their camps have disappeared. The picket line along the river is preserved, and as strong as ever... I am instructed to

BATTLE OF BRANDY STATION, 9 JUNE, 1863

Pleasonton hoped to cripple Stuart's Confederate cavalry with a swift raid. Approaching Brandy Station by several routes he hoped to box in and decimate the Southern cavalry. Poor coordination, luck and quick Confederate reaction allowed Stuart to drive Pleasonton off, but this action put the South on notice that the Union cavalry was now a force to be reckoned with.

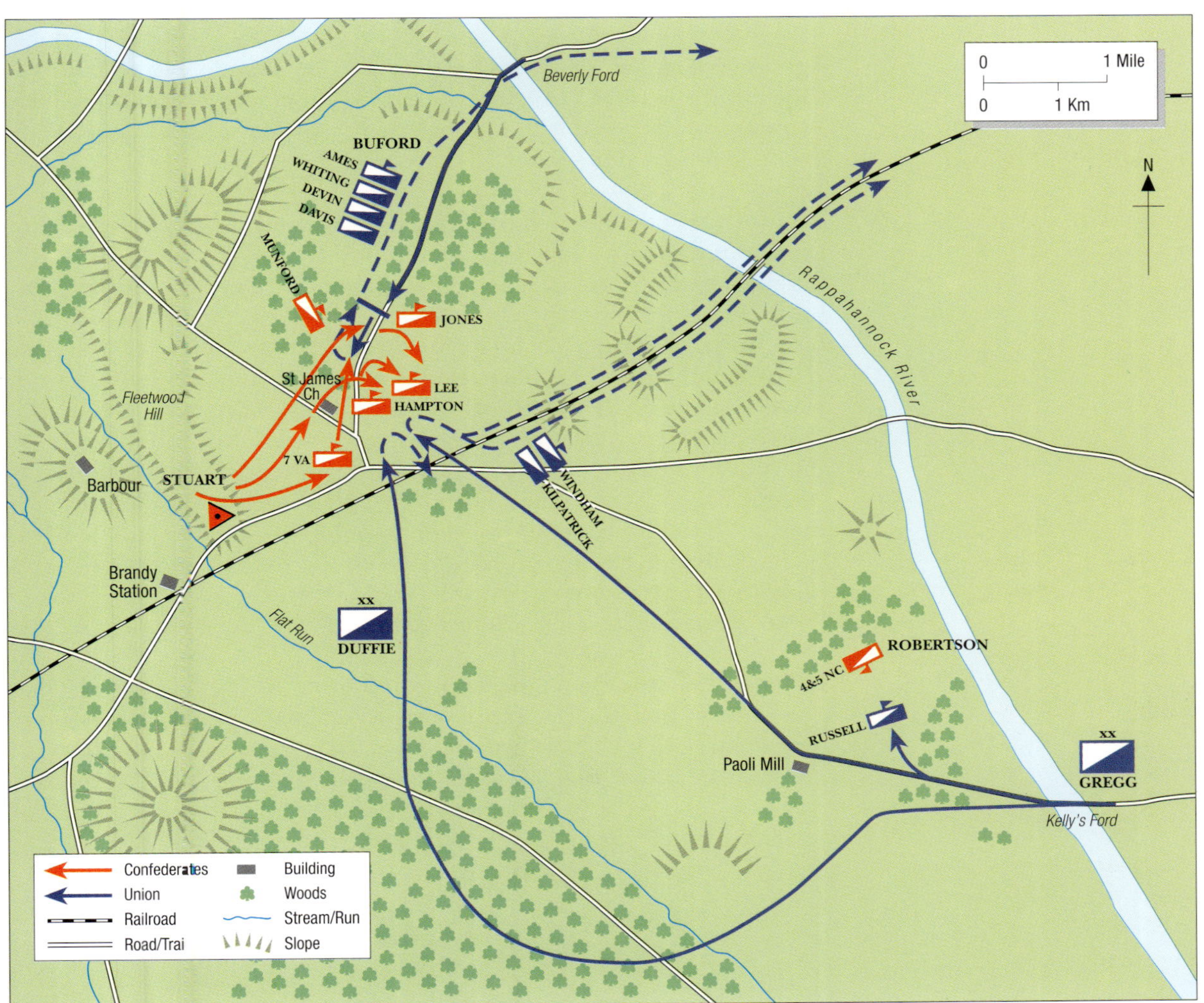

keep 'in view always the importance of covering Washington and Harpers Ferry.' In the event the enemy should move... the head of his column will probably be headed toward the Potomac via Gordonsville or Culpeper." (Hooker was correct in this.)

Halleck replies: "It would... seem perilous to permit Lee's main force to move upon the Potomac... Of course your movements must depend in great measure upon those made by Lee."

Hooker chafes at this ambivalence because he wants to attack the Confederate positions across the Rappahannock and push toward Richmond. He feels there are not enough Confederates in the area to stop an attack on the Confederate capital, but his superiors in Washington think he would do better to attack Lee's moving columns. While Hooker impatiently vacillates, J.E.B. Stuart's cavalry moves north to Brandy Station in keeping with Lee's plans.

6 June – J.E.B. Stuart parades nearly 8,000 Confederate cavalrymen gathered near Brandy Station for townsfolk and passengers in the railroad cars.

7 June – Lee reaches Culpeper.

8 June – Stuart holds a review for Lee and Gen. Hood's Texas infantry to show off his massed Confederate cavalry. Unknown to him, the Union Army knows where he is and has planned a surprise attack to cripple the Confederate cavalry.

9 June – Major-general Alfred Pleasonton sends nearly 10,000 Union cavalry in a pincer movement across Beverly and Kelly's fords on the Rappahannock to attack Stuart's camp. Brig-general John Buford leads three brigades of cavalry and one of infantry across Beverly's Ford, while both Brig.Gen. David McM. Gregg and Col. Alfred Duffie lead divisions across Kelly's Ford. This separation of troops prevents Pleasonton from massing his units in a crushing attack, and this, along with a little luck, saves Stuart. After a prolonged battle, the Union cavalry withdraws across the river and Stuart claims a victory. Still, many Southerners feel he was 'caught napping.' Although not immediately apparent to Southerners, the Union cavalry has come off well, fighting the famous J.E.B. Stuart to a standstill and gaining confidence which will help them at Gettysburg. Losses are 523 Confederate and 866 Federal casualties. One Confederate government official notes, "Stuart is... conceited... he got careless."

10 June – Ewell leaves Culpeper and moves north up the valley. Hooker again urges Lincoln to let him move on Richmond, believing it is unprotected since he feels Lee is moving his troops and massing them for a northern offensive. Lincoln reminds Hooker that his "true objective" is

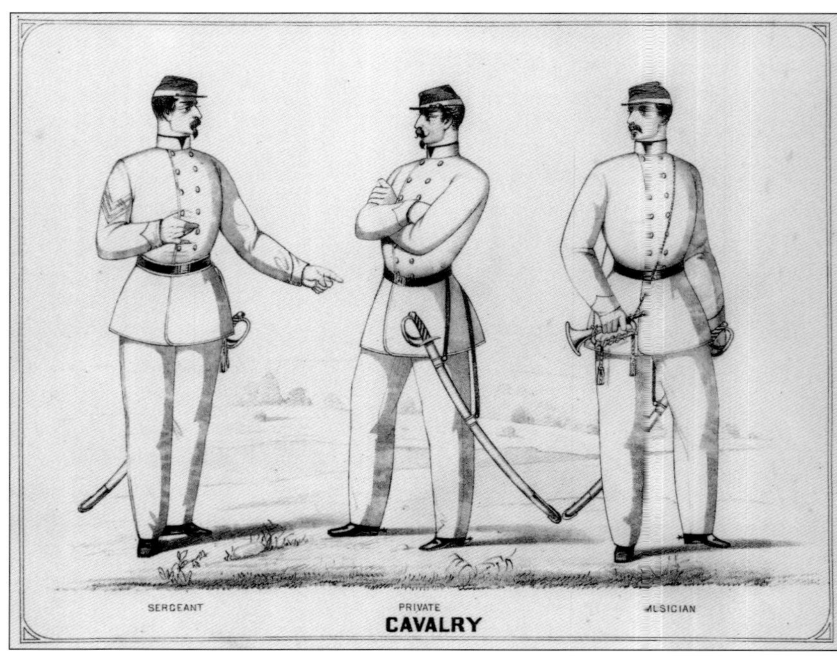

Confederate cavalry uniforms for the NCO, enlisted man, and musician. Similar to infantry dress, each branch of the service had distinctive cuff, chevron, collar, and kepi colors – in this case a light mustard yellow. As with Yankee uniforms, the French influence on style is obvious.

This field photograph shows the Union field hospital at Brandy Station. This area was fought over several times and just months earlier Union cavalry under Pleasonton had surprised Stuart here at the beginning of the Gettysburg campaign.

Lee's army, not Richmond. Hooker argues that, Lee "can leave nothing behind to interpose any serious obstacle to my rapid advance on Richmond... the most speedy and certain mode of giving the rebellion a mortal blow."

11 June – Halleck orders Hooker to guard against Lee and to not worry about Richmond as an objective. Hooker sends Sickles' III Corps (10,726 men) to Beverly's Ford near Brandy Station.

12 June – Ewell crosses the Blue Ridge Mountains and approaches Winchester. The Union commander at Winchester, General Milroy, misjudges the situation. He feels the skirmishes at Newtown, Cedarville and Middleton are just raids and are not a real threat, nor a serious Southern offensive. He bases this on intelligence gathered from captured Confederates. Unfortunately the latter were from units known to have been in the area. None of Ewell's men who were captured were questioned, so Milroy remained unaware of the real Southern threat.

Milroy's troops in Front Royal know of Ewell's presence but cannot communicate with Milroy because the telegraph lines have been cut between Front Royal and Winchester. However, even this does not alert Milroy to Ewell's presence. Scouts from the Union III Corps report Confederate pickets on the west bank of Beverly's Ford, and Hooker uneasily surmises that perhaps the Confederate Army is finally on the move.

13 June – Hooker leaves his position at Fredericksburg and begins to move the Army of the Potomac north, to the Manassas area. That same day Ewell takes Berryville and moves within a mile of the southern part of Winchester. The appearance of Ewell's army causes Milroy to retreat into the forts at Winchester.

Culpeper, Virginia, was on the Confederate route of march. Stuart held an impromptu cavalry parade for rail passengers on the Orange and Alexandria railroad near here, just before the Union surprise attack at Brandy Station.

14 June – Washington orders Milroy to abandon Winchester and withdraw to Harper's Ferry. Milroy delays, disagreeing because he does not think the Army of Northern Virginia can successfully evade Hooker's Army of the Potomac, which he knows is moving northward. His hesitation allows Ewell and Early to move into position and attack both Winchester and its outlying forts from the west, south and east. Suddenly anxious, Milroy abandons Winchester, wagons, and guns when he hears the road has been blocked, and his withdrawal becomes a foot race toward Maryland. At Fredericksburg, Hill is unopposed and follows Ewell and Longstreet north.

15 June – Milroy's troops arrive in Harper's Ferry.

16 June – Ewell crosses the Potomac at Williamsport, Maryland. The Army of the Potomac bivouacs throughout the Dumfries-Manassas-Fairfax area. Hooker asks Washington for reinforcements because he feels Lee is moving toward Washington, even though cavalry reconnaissance cannot discover the whereabouts of the Confederate Army. Lincoln and Halleck urge Hooker to move west, possibly as far as Harper's Ferry, to strike at where they believe Lee's army to be.

17 June – Pleasonton's cavalry runs into Stuart's men, both at Aldie and further west, at Middleburg, but cannot penetrate the Southern cavalry screen.

18 June – Hooker orders Pleasonton to find out what's behind the Confederate cavalry. Lee's generals continue their northward thrust and Stuart's cavalry holds the passes at Aldie, denying information to Hooker and confusing the Union high command.

19 June – Ewell moves closer to Pennsylvania while Longstreet and Hill advance through northern Virginia. Stuart clashes with Pleasonton at Middleburg.

W.E. 'Grumble' Jones saw the danger of an attack from Kelly's Ford, but when Stuart treated his admonition with disbelief, he muttered, "He thinks they ain't comin'; he'll damned soon see for himself."

As a precaution, Robertson's men were positioned at the first road north of Kelly's Ford, where Duffie crossed. Because the Federals got lost, they missed this road and went further west before turning north, missing Robertson's ambush entirely.

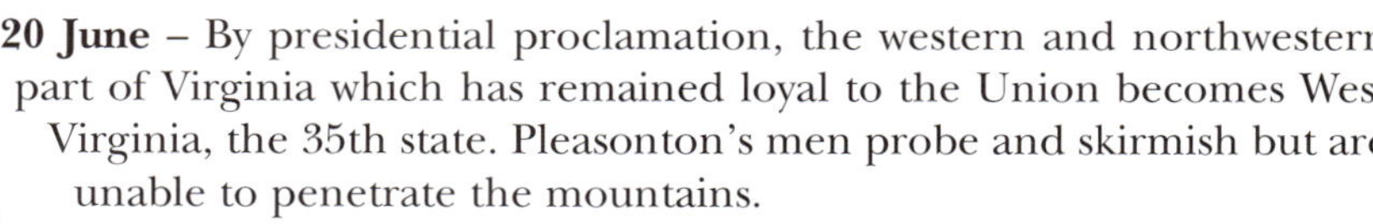

20 June – By presidential proclamation, the western and northwestern part of Virginia which has remained loyal to the Union becomes West Virginia, the 35th state. Pleasonton's men probe and skirmish but are unable to penetrate the mountains.

21 June – Union skirmishing at Gainesville, Haymarket, and Thoroughfare Gap fails to penetrate the mountains as the Army of Northern Virginia continues north.

22 June – Pleasonton captures some deserters and falls back to Aldie in the Bull Run Mountains, giving Hooker information which indicates that Lee, Longstreet, and Hill are following Ewell north. As these reports are based on interrogation of Confederate deserters, Hooker feels the information is suspect and does not act on it immediately. Confederate skirmishers are encountered at Greencastle, Pennsylvania.

23 June – Ewell moves north, while Longstreet and Hill are near the northernmost border of Virginia. Hooker travels to Washington, D.C. and meets with Halleck and Secretary of War Stanton to plead for more men.

24 June – Longstreet and Hill cross into Maryland, intent on linking up with Ewell. Hooker asks Washington for further orders, claiming he doesn't know his head from his feet with relation to Lee's position because of Stuart's successful screening.

25 June – Lee gives Stuart discretionary permission to move north. These orders give Stuart the latitude to prowl far and wide – ultimately arriving late at Gettysburg. Stuart is to go north between the Federal Army and Washington, D.C. and then swing west to form up with the Confederate Army near Harrisburg. Ewell's corps skirmishes with Federal troops near McConnellsburg, Pennsylvania. Lee, Longstreet, and Hill cross the Potomac at Williamsport. Hooker begins crossing into Maryland at Edward's Ferry.

Colonel Alfred Duffie's cavalry cut too far west before swinging north to follow Pleasonton's pincer plan and link up with Buford at Brandy Station to crush Stuart's cavalry between them.

26 June – General Early's command enters Gettysburg heading toward York, skirmishing with Federal militia, routing them, and capturing many in the process. General Hooker moves parts of his army toward Frederick, Maryland, while the rest are still on the other side of Edward's Ferry.

27 June – Hooker "advises" the evacuation of Union troops at Harper's Ferry because he wishes to strengthen his army by adding the commands at Harper's Ferry to it, declaring that he will step down from command of the Army of the Potomac if his advice is not taken. Lincoln, Halleck and Stanton confer, and decide to release Hooker from command of the Army of the Potomac. Meade is chosen as the new commander. Federal officers sent from Washington awaken Gen. George G. Meade before dawn on the 28th, making him think at first that he is being arrested. When told that he has been appointed as commander of the Army of the Potomac, Meade states that there are many better qualified and more deserving than he.

28 June – Meade receives orders from Lincoln and Halleck, officially appointing him commander of the Army of the Potomac at 0700 hours. Meade notes that he is not aware of the exact disposition "of the troops and the position of the enemy," but that he will place his army closer to the Susquehanna and between Lee's advancing troops and Washington or Baltimore.

Lee has planned an attack on Harrisburg, the capital of Pennsylvania, but changes his mind and orders Longstreet, Ewell, and Hill to disregard earlier objectives and move toward Gettysburg and Cashtown, almost 30 miles west of there, where he plans to make a stand. Early enters York and requisitions shoes, clothing, rations, and $100,000. General John Gordon is given a note by a Southern sympathizer which describes the positions and strength of Union troops in Wrightsville. When Confederate forces move on Wrightsville, Union troops attempt to deny them entry to the city by blowing up a bridge. The explosion fails, prompting the Union troops to set fire to the bridge, setting fire to Wrightsville in the process. Confederates help the locals quell the fire while the Union Army escapes. Stuart captures a 125-wagon Federal supply train near Rockville, Maryland, unaware of the proximity of the Army of the Potomac to either himself or the Confederate Army. Longstreet's scout tells him the Union Army is close – he shared a meal with them earlier in the day! Lee's original plan was to fight at Cashtown with the mountains protecting his back and flanks,

Cavalry were the eyes and ears of both armies, acting as spies, scouts, and intelligence-gathering branches as well as pickets, outriders and mounted flankers. This Union cavalry is stopping at a farmhouse near Gettysburg.

Judson Kilpatrick was a pugnacious cavalry commander who was personally fearless and believed nothing could deter his cavalry. He threw his men into battle with such reckless abandon that he was nicknamed "Kill-cavalry."

not at Gettysburg, but events are changing his plans, although he is unaware of the exact location of the Union Army.

29 June – Stuart raids Sykesville and cuts Union telegraph lines, which alerts the Union Army to Stuart's presence to their northeast. At the Susquehanna, Ewell receives Lee's orders and turns back towards Gettysburg. Pausing barely long enough to put on his hat, Meade orders his forces north through Maryland, sending almost a third of the Army of the Potomac hurrying towards Gettysburg. En route he assesses the situation and begins formulating a plan with options that depend upon where the Army of Northern Virginia is finally located.

By evening, the Union Army has positioned its left at Emmitsburg and secured its right at New Windsor. General Judson Kilpatrick and Gen. Custer's cavalry move west from Hanover to cover the Union flank, encountering Stuart heading towards Harrisburg. Stuart beats them off and, unaware of the situation now developing at Gettysburg because he is out of touch with Lee, follows his original plan, moving north to rendezvous with Ewell and Early, not realizing they have already turned back from the Susquehanna.

30 June – Ordered to proceed to Gettysburg, Gen. Buford's cavalry moves north on the Taneytown Road to Gettysburg, travels straight up Washington Street, turns west on the Chambersburg Pike and moves across to the seminary. Buford establishes skirmish lines west of town, less than four miles from Hill's advancing troops. Ewell leaves York and heads towards Gettysburg, while Confederate troops at Chambersburg move east to converge on Gettysburg. Meade orders General Reynolds to occupy Gettysburg and reinforce Buford's cavalry. Confederate Gen. Henry Heth learns from Pettigrew, who was in Gettysburg three days earlier, that he encountered no Federals there. So Heth decides to take his troops to obtain badly needed shoes that are rumoured to be warehoused in Gettysburg.

Thus, the stage was set.

OPPOSING COMMANDERS

The commanders and men who met at Gettysburg were as different as night and day. Not only were they from a mixture of rural and urban communities, but some were privileged, others farmers, woodsmen, hunters, and horsemen; still others were tradesmen or labourers who had never held a gun before.

Confederate leader: Robert E. Lee

Lee was a career soldier, related to the oldest and best known families in the United States. An officer in the Mexican-American War, he had been superintendent of West Point and had led the marines which captured John Brown at Harper's Ferry and had either taught or served with many of the men who wore blue or gray. Offered command of the United States Armed Forces, Lee deliberated and then turned the position down for one reason alone: he was a Virginian first and an American second. To him, his state of birth was his primary allegiance. His viewpoint was not unusual in the days of newspapers which were months old and telegraphs whose service was erratic at best, and all news was weighed against its local impact to ascertain its importance. Lee was not pro-slavery, and everyone who spoke of him referred to him as a gentleman in word and deed in the truest sense. He was educated, compassionate, intellectual and somewhat reserved, and he was highly thought of by all who came into contact with him – a man of principle and conviction. Choosing to serve Virginia instead of the United States was not an easy decision.

As a professional soldier, Lee was trained in the tactics of Napoleon, but the Mexican-American War and subsequent events had taught him several things about real war. He was bold and inventive, and had faith in his men. He took educated risks in forming battle plans, but was never foolhardy or reckless with the lives of the men he commanded; in fact, he was a man who listened to soldiers of all ranks and from all stations of life and considered their viewpoints and opinions. In return, his troops had faith in him which bordered almost on reverence. Next to Stonewall Jackson, he was the most aggressive commander the South had and respected by all. As a commander at West Point, he had helped train many younger officers on both sides.

Lee gave his subordinates room to exercise initiative. If he had a failing, perhaps it was this latitude he gave his commanders, since not all of them exercised the caution or boldness which he expected. Prior to Chancellorsville, the Army of Northern Virginia had been a perfectly balanced machine, with Jackson an aggressive and somewhat impetuous

Robert E. Lee was the most respected commander in either army, having served in Mexico and at West Point, and having led the attack on Harper's Ferry to capture John Brown. He turned down command of the Union Army to serve his home state of Virginia.

and inventive corps commander and Longstreet a more cautious and methodical one. Following Jackson's death, Lee's comfortable command structure was shattered. Lee's command style was to issue overall orders or directives and then leave the exact manner of execution up to his subordinates. With Longstreet and Jackson everyone knew how one another thought and could reasonably guess how they would react, but with the introduction of Ewell and Hill as new corps commanders, uncertainty crept in the door.

Lee was not at his physical best at Gettysburg, as evidenced by his lack of ready plans and vacillation. His health was failing, and he was aware of this. Heart disease had already weakened him and a riding accident had damaged his hands earlier. However, part of his general lack of preparation must be attributed to Hill, who precipitated a battle which he had been told not to start without Lee's express command. Lee had a plan which called for the Confederate Army to assemble at Cashtown with the mountains protecting its rear and make the Army of the Potomac move toward them. The illness of Hill and the brashness of Heth catapulted the Army of Northern Virginia into an engagement which Lee had expressly forbidden. However, the engagement escalated until he had no choice but to meet the enemy or fight a disastrous withdrawing action. That Lee made three attacks at different points on the Union lines on three different days has been cited as lack of a plan, but it is no sign of his failure as a commander, for Lee had no cavalry to tell him what he faced and so was testing the line to see if he could find a weak point. The intelligence he lacked would have informed him that Meade was shuttling Union troops back and forth to reinforce points in the line where they were needed.

Aware of his frailty and the growing strength and competence of the Union forces, Lee felt time was running out for him and for his beloved Virginia. He acted boldly at Gettysburg because boldness would put the Union on the defensive and that would help the Southern cause. If Lee could have defeated the Union decisively at Gettysburg, he would have died a happy man, because such a Union defeat would have brought respite for Virginia or ended the war. As it was, there were two long years of warfare ahead. After the war, Lee became president of what is now Washington and Lee University and lived barely five years past Appomattox.

George Gordon Meade was an organized commander who after his appointment as commander of the Army of the Potomac had two days to familiarize himself with his new command before engaging Lee at Gettysburg.

Union leader: George Gordon Meade

George Gordon Meade was a good general, perhaps much better than history allows. Like Lee, he was a career soldier and a devoted family man. Unlike Lee, he had a terrible sudden temper and sharp tongue when someone aroused his ire, and he did not hesitate to show it. However, he could be considerate and compassionate to his subordinates when the need arose. He too had served with many of the Confederate commanders and his subordinate Union commanders in earlier days, and he knew their strengths and weaknesses. Having recently been a corps commander, he was used to paying attention to detail and seeing that all the nuances of plans were carried out as assigned. If there was one major difference between Meade and Lee, this was it: when given the news that he had been appointed com-

General Meade with his headquarters officers and Army of the Potomac corps and division commanders. Standing on the far right is a foreign military observer in uniform, distinguished by his shoulder sash and undress garrison cap.

mander of the Army of the Potomac, Meade's first response was that there were many others better suited to command – his second was to familiarize himself with every unit's position, readiness and strength.

Meade gave orders that were precise and well detailed, for he was a methodical and careful commander. As Gettysburg showed, he was quick to adapt to the changing necessities of combat where strategies were concerned, while many of his contemporaries were one-trick ponies. From the time he verbally accepted command of the Army of the Potomac, at 0300 hours on 28 June, 1863, until the clash at Gettysburg, he barely had 48 hours to assess the capabilities of his army, devise a battle plan, oversee logistics, and put his army into motion to find and stop the Army of Northern Virginia. Aware of Lincoln's admonitions to find the Southerners and bring them into battle and destroy them, he gave that his full attention.

Few other commanders could have done what Meade did in not only preparing to meet the Confederate onslaught, but accepting command and improvising strategies while on the move. He freely used the strengths and talents of others around him, such as Reynolds, Howard, Doubleday, Slocum and Warren, to prepare the Union Army for its greatest test. That any should criticize him for lack of a speedy follow-up after the devastating battle at Gettysburg is typical of 'armchair generals', far removed from the scene of combat and the realities of the battlefield. There is the very real possibility that every Union soldier at Gettysburg was shell-shocked after the relentless three days of carnage. Very few men could do what Meade accomplished at Gettysburg, and one of those few happened to be in command of the other side.

The cavalry commanders

When one considers J.E.B. Stuart, Alfred Pleasonton, Judson Kilpatrick, Wade Hampton, and George Armstrong Custer, one looks at cavalrymen who would have been at home as hussars in the armies of Napoleon or Wellington. They were personally fearless, tactically aggressive, and incapable of understanding the larger picture and strategy, sometimes to the point of recklessness. Although personable, these men were impulsive and vainglorious, as Stuart showed with his long ride that left the Army of Northern Virginia blind and without intelligence and as Custer showed throughout his career which culminated at Little Big Horn but could have done so at any juncture in his career had he been less lucky. To a man, they aggressively met battlefield situations head-on. Lee thought highly of Stuart, but he realized Stuart's failings and knew that Stuart needed a firm hand to guide and give strategic direction.

Stuart was fond of uniforms, almost to the point of being a dandy. He loved banjo music and had a musician accompany him almost everywhere he campaigned. He was an excellent horseman, a dashing gentleman, and a devoted husband and father. He was one of the Confederacy's most able commanders, and his death in 1864 left a void impossible to fill.

On the other side of the coin were cavalry commanders like John Buford and McIntosh. Buford was a proponent of what would be called 'blitzkrieg' nearly a century later. As far as he was concerned, infantry walked and cavalry rode to battle, but once there, they both fought on foot. Buford knew tactics and understood strategy, aware that cavalrymen armed with faster-firing breechloading carbines and Colt six-shot .44 revolvers could delay a superior enemy's advance. With any number of other cavalry commanders at Gettysburg in that first meeting with Heth, a charge and blaze of glory would have stunned the Confederates, who would then have formed battle lines and blasted the riders into oblivion, and the net result would have been that Reynolds would have had to enter Gettysburg whistling Dixie if he was to enter at all.

Other Union commanders

Gettysburg highlights the best and the worst traits of commanders and the men they led. Without men of vision like Buford, Reynolds, Vincent, Chamberlain, Howard, Warren, and Meade, the North would have lost at Gettysburg. Without capable commanders like Lee, Longstreet, Hood, Pettigrew, Early, and Law, the Confederacy would have withered and faded after those three days of slaughter.

Reynolds' death could have been a fatal blow to the Union if men such as Howard and Hancock had not been there to take command and keep unthinking commanders such as Sickles in line. Hancock had a knack for being in the right place at the right time, and he always managed to have a clean white shirt to wear with his uniform, no matter what the battlefield conditions or the distance from base. Hancock was a soldier's soldier who knew not only what the right thing to do was, but when to do it, and how. Joshua Chamberlain was a college teacher of oratory. He put this to use when rallying his troops, preferring to sway them rather than bluntly order them, realizing that volunteers were different from career soldiers. His decisiveness and bold charge on Little Round Top may have been the action which saved the Union on 2 July.

General Daniel Butterfield deserves credit not just for the rank and position he held (chief-of-staff), but for the practical changes he implemented. Today his name is obscured by many, but his actions affected every soldier in the army from Gettysburg to the present day. With Hooker he introduced standardized corps badges so soldiers from different corps and different divisions could be differentiated by the color of their badges. He is also credited with introducing a number of bugle calls during the civil war, among them Taps.

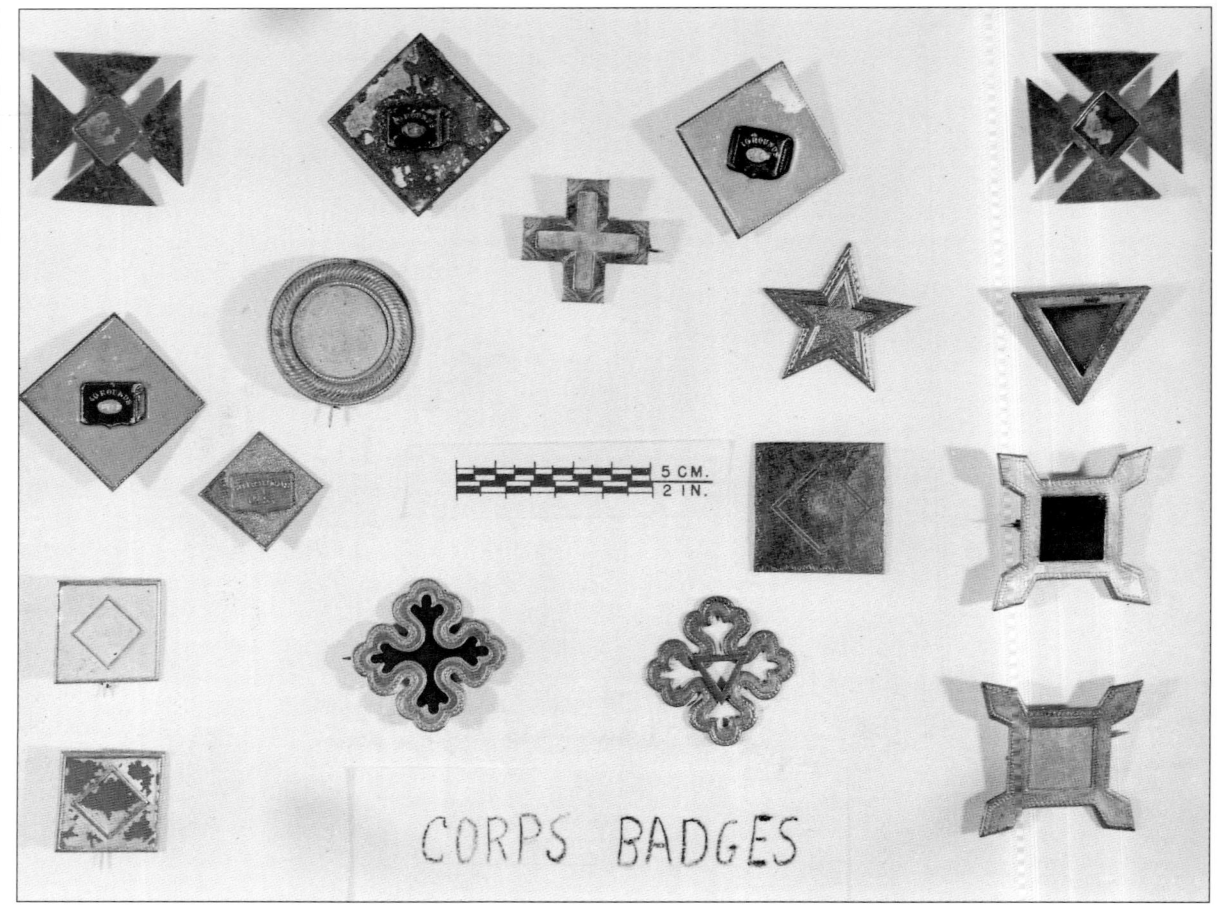

The Union Army adopted distinctive hat corps badges in 1863: I, circle; II, clover leaf; III, diamond; V, Maltese cross; VI, straight cross; XI, crescent; and XII, five-pointed star. 1st division emblem was always red; 2nd, white; and 3rd, blue.

Lee's commanders

James Longstreet was a favourite of Lee, called "Old Pete" or "Old Warhorse." Lee depended upon him and trusted Longstreet's judgement. He valued Longstreet's opinion (even when it differed from his own) and listened to his counsel before making decisions. Longstreet was suffering the personal loss of three of his children, who had died of fever in Richmond in 1862. He was a calculating and cautious commander who believed in defensive warfare and thought no battle was better than one where the enemy dashed himself to bits against your prepared fortifications.

Richard ("Old Baldy") Ewell was one of Jackson's commanders and had earlier lost a leg. He had been Lee's choice to command Jackson's II corps. Although his leg wound had healed, he was hesitant at Gettysburg. Even though his troops were very successful on 1 July he was slow to follow up on an opportunity that could have won the day when it presented itself. When he finally decided to commit, Lee stopped him, knowing that the moment had passed, even if Ewell did not.

Jubal Early chewed tobacco, suffered from arthritis, and cursed freely, even in Lee's presence. Lee referred to him as "My Bad Old Man," but had confidence in this earthy, no-nonsense commander. Early passed through Gettysburg on his way to York and demanded ransom, but goods were hidden and little was given. He passed word back, and it eventually reached Hill and Heth. At Wrightsville Early's troops helped locals put out the fire which threatened to burn down the town after the fleeing Union troops tried to burn the bridge they had failed to blow up. A.P. Hill was an erratic commander. When he felt well, he commanded well, but he was often ill. At Gettysburg he was sick, and many have speculated that his illness was psychosomatic. Robertson speculates Hill suffered from syphillis contracted in his West Point days.

Perhaps the most tragic figure at Gettysburg is George Pickett. Unfortunately his name has been sullied by association with the charge which he led that now bears his name. Yet Pickett was a capable commander. He was neither the brightest nor the most clever (having come at the bottom of his class at West Point), but he was a soldier who had a way with his men, and he followed orders. The charge across the fields of Gettysburg on 3 July, 1863, was primarily his unit. However, he had not chosen who was to charge: Longstreet had. Longstreet had not chosen to attack that point, Lee had, and Longstreet sent Pickett's unit simply because it was fresh, and was most apt to succeed against the Union lines. How deeply Pickett felt about the charge was revealed in a meeting with Lee after the war, when he told a comrade that "that old man [Lee] cost him his division."

Analysis

As stated, A.P. Hill was ill at Gettysburg, and his lack of strict attention to Lee's orders may have been in part due to his condition. The worst that can be said of Hill is that he was professional and somewhat unimaginative. Many have unfavourably compared Hill and Ewell to Jackson, but this is like comparing Napoleonic commanders to Wellington or Bonaparte, or armour commanders to Patton – there simply are not many who can do what these men did, so such comparisons fall short of the mark. Ewell was timid, and as yet uncertain how to manage a corps, and his performance at Gettysburg was less than many would have expected of him, especially his failure on the first day to follow up and seize the hills south of town. Instead he hesitated, and his hesitation gave the Union time to reorganize.

Reynolds was perhaps the best hope of what might have been. His brief spurt of glory allowed the Union to solidify a defence, and he died before he could make a mistake. Hancock, Howard, Warren, and Slocum showed inventiveness and an ability to work with others to achieve a goal; all had the respect of their men, which increased their effectiveness. After Reynolds, Hancock was perhaps the next most impressive commander, because his efforts on July 3rd helped turn the tide against the Confederacy.

THE OPPOSING ARMIES

What is true of the commanders at Gettysburg is also true of their men: they were a mixed lot – of good and bad, capable and incapable – who acted upon their beliefs as best they could and individually volunteered their last full measure to those beliefs. By 1863 Confederate resources were strained to the limit. Southern soldiers wore replacement butternut (yellow-brown, a substitute for gray) clothing, original issue uniforms were in tatters, men wore homespun clothes, shoes and boots were worn out and had not usually been replaced, and often the only way to tell a Southern soldier from a farmer was the soldier's ever-present rifle, cartridge box, canteen, and blanket roll.

The most common rifles were the Enfield .577 caliber rifle and the Springfield .58 musket, although some Dixie armouries turned out passable imitations of Colt (Leech & Rigdon, and Griswold & Gunnison) and Remington (Spiller & Burr) revolvers as well as the newer Sharps breech-loading rifle. In close combat many muskets fired 'buck and ball,' a combination of a ball and two to six buckshot. Sometimes muskets in close quarters were loaded with buckshot and used as shotguns.

Many Southerners had been at war for three years and were hardened to life in the field. Those "twelve-month men" who started the war had either re-enlisted or had long since gone home to their hard-scrabble farms. Coffee was nonexistent, and chicory (a bitter, though passable, ersatz) was its most common substitute. Men ate cornmeal 'Johnny cakes' (cornmeal cooked in a skillet by 'Johnny Rebs,' which was so prevalent that it took its name from the men who ate it), and they scrounged off the land, eating greens (dandelion, collards, kale, and turnip greens) when they were in season and going through wild fruits and berries like a horde of foraging bears.

Most soldiers carried haversacks and blanket rolls; very few Southerners carried knapsacks or backpacks. Cavalry were usually armed with sabers and shotguns, although some also carried cap and ball revolvers. Carbines were much less prevalent among Confederate cavalry than with their Union counterparts. Despite continuous short food supplies, privation, and materiel shortages of almost every kind, these soldiers were at their peak: lean, mean fighting machines, to steal a phrase used a hundred years later.

Union forces were better supplied than the Southerners. The long frock coat and Hardee hat of the early war had given way to a shorter field blouse, and units wore either kepis or slouch hats. Preferences for knapsacks, haversacks, and blanket rolls were evenly divided. The common rifle was the US Army model 1861 Springfield .58 caliber rifle musket, although two special units of Sharpshooter carried the Sharps breech-loading rifle. The most common round ball had given way to the Minie ball, a conical bullet capable of tearing large holes in its target. Cavalry were armed with saber, revolver and (commonly, by this time) a Sharps breech-loading carbine; some units even had the new Spencer 7-shot carbine, which was loaded by inserting a seven-round tubular magazine into the butt of the rifle. Those armed with Spencer carbines carried additional tubes pre-loaded in a special cartridge box, but the tubes were easily bent, causing the weapon to malfunction. In one instance, during the fight for Bloody Angle, Union troops loaded their muskets with buckshot and fired into the Confederates to break up their charge.

There were some Union logistical problems, but these were generally localized and not widespread: as a rule, Union troops were better fed and supplied than Southern troops, and the privations they suffered were more of a temporary than a permanent nature. Although sometimes out of supply, coffee was so common that each Union company had one man issued a 'coffee grinder' Sharps. This had a special coffee mill built into its stock with a removable handle, so troops could grind their own beans.

Many Union troops carried haversacks with extra socks, heavy overcoats, blankets, gum-blankets (a waterproof groundsheet), canteens, cups, and leggings or heavy wool socks which they could pull up over their trouser legs. Because of more prevalent conscription, many Union troops were at first less hardened than their Confederate counterparts, but in general the quality of the Union soldier was much improved as troops from the Midwest bolstered the stalwart farm boys, fishermen, millworkers, and city dwellers to give the Yankees a much more battle-ready force. By this stage of the war, the Southern superiority of outdoorsmen and hunters was waning, and Union troops were much better trained than they had been at the start of the war.

Uniforms of both sides showed the influence of French military dress. North and South had Zouaves at Gettysburg (the 14th New York and the Louisiana Tiger Zouaves), and the chasseur-style coat and shell jacket, as well as the kepi, were common-issue on both sides. In 1863 the Union Army adopted their different colored corps badges, worn on their hats to identify each unit and each division within a corps. The first division's badge was red; the second division's, white; and the third's, blue. Previously there had usually simply been crossed rifles for infantry, cannon barrels for artillery and sabers for cavalry. Most Union equipment was marked 'US' or 'USA,' and Confederate equipment was marked 'CSA.' Some Texas units wore a single star to signify that they were from the 'Lone Star State.'

With three years of war behind them, North and South boasted professional armies. Both sides had a mix of experienced soldiers who would stand fast in the face of their enemies. Gettysburg would test their mettle.

GETTYSBURG ORDER OF BATTLE

The order of battle contains the units, names of commanders, and estimated or actual number of effectives (number of men engaged in combat, not those on TDY, injured, furloughed and so on), and in the case of artillery units, followed by a code which is the number of guns of each type in a unit. In cases where units were assigned but not present, they are not included in the total of men who were engaged from that unit. Whenever possible unit strength reports were used. In some cases strength has been extrapolated from quarter master or other rolls.

ABBREVIATIONS

Abbreviations of rank: **Maj.Gen.** = Major-general, **Lt.Gen.** = Lieutenant-general, **Brig.Gen.** = Brigadier-general, **Col.** = Colonel, **Lt.Col.** = Lieutenant-colonel **Maj.** = Major, **Capt.** = Captain, **1st Lt.** = 1st Lieutenant, and, **2nd Lt.** = 2nd Lieutenant.

Abbreviations for types of artillery pieces are: **N**=Napoleon gun, **6G**=6lb. field gun, **10H**=10lb. howitzer, **12H**=12lb. howitzer, **20H**=20lb. howitzer, **24H**=24lb. howitzer, **3R**=3-inch rifle, **4.5R**=4.5-inch rifle, **10P**=10lb. Parrott rifle, **20P**=20lb. Parrott rifle, **JR**=James Rifle, **W**= Whitworth gun, **BR**=Blakely Rifle, **3NR**=3-inch Navy Rifle

GETTYSBURG ORDER OF BATTLE JULY 1ST, 1863

ARMY OF THE POTOMAC

Maj.Gen. George G. Meade
(112,735 total; 95,799 engaged)

General HQ: Provost Marshall Gen.:
Brig.Gen. Marsena R. Patrick (1,528)
Guards & Orderlies: Oneida New York Cavalry:
Capt. Daniel P. Mann (42)
Attached: Gen. Gouvenor K. Warren
Field & Staff Officers: 8

93RD NEW YORK (DETACHMENTS)
Col. John S. Crocker (148)
8th US Inf. – Capt. Edwin W.H. Reed (at Taneytown, MD) (401)
2nd Pennsylvania Cavalry – Col. R. Butler Prue (489)
6th Pennsylvania, Cos E & I – Capt. James Starr (81)
Reg. Cavalry Detachments, 1,2,5, & 6 Regt.'s (15)
Signal Corps – Capt. Lemuel B. Norton (51)
Artillery – Brig.Gen. Henry J. Hunt

ENGINEERS (not at Gettysburg):
15th New York
50th New York
US Battalion of Engineers

I CORPS

Maj.Gen. John F. Reynolds (Maj.Gen. Abner Doubleday, Maj.Gen. John Newton) (12,596)

General HQ: L/1st Maine Cavalry – Lt.Col. Charles H. Smith (57)
B/121st Pennsylvania – Maj. Alexander Biddle (306)
Field & Staff Officers: 14

1ST DIVISION

Brig.Gen. James S. Wadsworth (3,860)
Field & Staff Officers: 11

1ST BRIGADE (Iron Brigade):
Brig.Gen. Solomon Meredith (Col.Wm. W. Robinson) (1,829 engaged)
Field & Staff Officers/Band: 15
2nd Wisconsin – Col. Lucius Fairchild (302)
6th Wisconsin – Lt.Col. Rufus L. Dawes (Iron Bde.) (344)
7th Wisconsin – Col. Wm. W. Robinson (364)
19th Indiana – Col. Samuel J. Williams (308)
24th Michigan – Col. Henry A. Morrow (496)

2ND BRIGADE:
Brig.Gen. Lysander Cutler (2,020)
Field & Staff Officers/Band: 17
84th New York (14th Brooklyn Militia) – Col. Edw. B. Fowler (318)
147th New York – Lt.Col. Francis C. Miller (380)
76th New York – Maj. Andrew J. Grover (375)
95th New York – Col. George H. Biddle (241)
56th Pennsylvania – Col. J. Wm. Hoffman (252)
7th Indiana – Col. Ira G. Grover (437)

2ND DIVISION

Brig.Gen. John C. Robinson (3,027)
Field & Staff Officers: 3

1ST BRIGADE:
Brig.Gen. Gabriel R. Paul (1,829)
94th New York – Col. Adrian R. Root (411)
104th New York – Col. Gilbert G. Prey (309)
11th Pennsylvania – Col. Richard Colter (trf fr 2nd Bde) (292)
107th Pennsylvania – Lt.Col. James MacThompson (255)
16th Maine – Col. Charles G. Tolden (298)
13th Massachusetts – Col. Samuel H. Leonard (284)

2ND BRIGADE:
Maj.Gen. Henry Baxter (1,198)
Field & Staff Officers: 4
12th Massachusetts – Col. James L. Bates (261)
83rd New York (9th Militia) Lt.Col. Joseph A. Moesch (215)
97th New York – Col. Charles Wheelock (236)
88th Pennsylvania – Maj. Benezet F. Foust (274)
90th Pennsylvania – Col. Peter Lyle (208)

3RD DIVISION

Maj.Gen.Abner Doubleday (Brig.Gen. Thomas A. Rowley) (4,711)
Provost Guard: **Co D 149th Pennsylvania** – Col. Walton Dwight (60)

1ST BRIGADE:
Brig.Gen. T. Rowley (Col.Chapman Biddle) (1,387)
Field & Staff Officers: 8
80th New York – Col. Theodore B. Gates (287)
121st Pennsylvania – Maj. Alexander Biddle (263)
142nd Pennsylvania – Col. Robert P. Cummins (362)
151st Pennsylvania – Lt.Col. George F. McFarland (467)

2ND BRIGADE (Bucktail Brigade):
Col. Roy Stone (1,314)
Field & Staff Officers: 2
143rd Pennsylvania – Col. Edward L. Dana (465)
149th Pennsylvania – Lt.Col. Walton Dwight (450)
150th Pennsylvania – Col. Langhorne Wister (397)

3RD BRIGADE:
Brig.Gen. Geo. T. Stannard (1,950)
Field & Staff Officers: 6
12th Vermont – Col. Asa P. Blount (guarding baggage) (641)
13th Vermont – Col. Francis V. Randall (636)
14th Vermont – Col. Wm. T. Nichols (647)
15th Vermont – Col. Redfield Proctor (guarding baggage) (637)
16th Vermont – Col. Wheelock G. Veazey (661)

I CORPS ARTILLERY BRIGADE:
Col. Chas. S. Wainwright (621)
Field & Staff Officers: 7
B Btty 2nd Maine Btty – Capt. James A. Hall (117) (6/3R)
E/5th Maine Lt. Btty – Capt. Greenleaf T. Stevens (119) (6/N)
B/1st Penn. Lt. Arty – Capt. James H. Cooper (114) (4/3R)
E&L/1st New York Lt. Arty – Capt. Gilbert H. Reynolds (141) (6/3R)
B Btty 4th US – 1st Lt. James Stewart (123) (6/N)

II CORPS

Maj.Gen.Winfield Scott Hancock (Brig.Gen. John Gibbon; July 3rd – Brig.Gen. Wm. Hays) (11,509)

General HQ: **6th New York Cavalry/D&K** – Capt. Riley Johnson (64)
Cos A, B, K 53rd Pennsylvania – Lt.Col. Richards McMichael (70)
Field & Staff Officers: 6

1ST DIVISION

Brig.Gen. John C. Caldwell (3,400)

Provost Guard: **Co. B 116th Pennsylvania** – Lt.Col. St. Clair Agustin Mullholland (32)
53rd Pennsylvania – Lt.Col. Richard McMichael (70)
Field & Staff Officers: 7

1ST BRIGADE:
Col. E.E. Cross (932)
Field & Staff Officers: 3
81st Pennsylvania – Col.Boyd McKean (175)
148th Pennsylvania – Lt.Col. Robert MacFarlane (468)
5th New Hampshire – Lt.Col. Chas. E. Hapgood (182)
61st New York – Lt.Col. K. Oscar Broady (104)

2ND BRIGADE :
Col.Patrick Kelly (532)
Field & Staff Officers: 2
63rd New York – Lt.Col. Richard C. Beutley (75)
69th New York – Capt. Richard Moroney (75)
116th Pennsylvania – Lt.Col. St. Clair A. Mulholland (66)
88th New York – Capt. Denis F. Burke (90)
28th Massachusetts – Col. R. Byrnes (224)

3RD BRIGADE:
Brig.Gen. Samuel K. Zook (975)
Field & Staff Officers: 4
52nd New York – Lt.Col. C.G. Freudenberg (134)
57th New York – Lt.Col. Alford B. Chapman (175)
66th New York – Col. Orlando H. Morris (147)
140th Pennsylvania – Col. Richard P. Roberts (515)

4TH BRIGADE:
Col. John R. Brook (852)
Field & Staff Officers: 1
53rd Pennsylvania – Lt.Col. Richard McMichael (136)
145th Pennsylvania – Col. Hiram K. Brown (202)
27th Connecticut – Lt.Col. Henry C. Merwin (75)
64th New York – Col. Daniel C. Bingham (204)
2nd Delaware – Col. Wm. P. Bailey (234)

2ND DIVISION

Brig.Gen. John F. Gibbon (Brig.Gen. William F. Harrow) (3,606)

Provost Guard: **Co. C 1st Minnesota** – Brig.Gen. Wm. F. Harrow (56)
Unattached: **1st Massachusetts Sharpshooters** – Capt. Wm. Plumer (42)

1ST BRIGADE:
Brig.Gen. Wm. F. Harrow (1,378)

19th Maine – Col. Francis E. Heath (439)
15th Massachusetts – Col. George H. Ward (239)
82nd New York (2nd Militia) – Lt.Col. James Houston (335)
1st Minnesota (2nd Minnesota Sharpshooters attached) – Col. Wm. Covill Jr. (330) Co L (32)

2ND BRIGADE:
Brig.Gen. Alexander S. Webb (1,208)
Field & Staff Officers: 3
69th Pennsylvania – Col. Dennis O'Kane (284)
71st Pennsylvania – Col. Richard Penn-Smith (261)
72nd Pennsylvania – Col. DeWitt C. Baxter (380)
106th Pennsylvania – Lt.Col. Wm. L. Curry (280)

3RD BRIGADE:
Col.Norman J. Hall (922)
Field & Staff Officers: 2
19th Massachusetts – Col. Arthur F. Devereaux (163)
20th Massachusetts – Col. Paul J. Revere (243)
7th Michigan – Lt.Col. Amos E. Steele Jr. (165)
42nd New York – Col. James E. Mallon (197)
59th New York – Lt.Col. Max A. Thomond (152)

3RD DIVISION

Brig.Gen. Alexander Hays (3,760)
Provost Guard: **10th New York Bttn.** – Maj.Gen. F. Hopper (82)

1ST BRIGADE:
Col.Samuel S. Carroll (1,036)
Field & Staff Officers: 1
Provost Guard: **8th Ohio and detached troops** – Capt. Alfred Craig (36)
4th Ohio – Lt.Col. Leonard W. Carpenter (229)
8th Ohio – Lt.Col. Franklin Sawyer (209)
14th Indiana – Col. John Coons (236)
7th West Virginia – Lt.Col. Jonathan H. Lockwood (319)

2ND BRIGADE:
Col.Thomas A. Smyth (1,134)
Field & Staff Officers: 2
14th Connecticut – Maj. Theodore G. Ellis (200)
1st Delaware – Lt.Col. Edward P. Harris (288)
12th New Jersey – Maj. John T. Hill (444)
108th New York – Lt.Col. Francis E. Pierce (200)

3RD BRIGADE:
Col. George L. Willard (1,508)
Field & Staff Officers: 2
39th New York – Maj. Hugo Hildebrandt (269)
111th New York – Col. Clinton D. MacDougall (390)
125th New York – Lt.Col. Levin Crandall (392)
126th New York – Col. Eliakim Sherrill (455)

II CORPS ARTILLERY BRIGADE
Capt. J.G. Hazard (603)
Field & Staff Officers: 4
A/1st Rhode Island – Capt. Wm. A. Arnold (117) (6/3R)
B/1st Rhode Island – 1st Lt. T. Fred Brown (129) (6/N)
A/4th US Arty – 1st Lt. Alonzo H. Cushing (126) (6/3R)
I/1st US Arty – 1st Lt. George A. Woodruff (113) (6/N)
B/1st New York Lt. Arty (14th New York Btty attached) – 1st Lt. Albert S. Sheldon (114) (6/3R)

III CORPS

Maj.Gen. Daniel E. Sickles (Maj.Gen. David B. Birney) (10,726)
General HQ: **A/6th New York Cavalry** – Maj. Wm. E. Beardsley (51)

1ST DIVISION

Maj.Gen.David B. Birney (Brig.Gen. J.H. Hobart Ward) (5,090)
Field & Staff Officers: 4

1ST BRIGADE:
Brig.Gen. Chas. K. Graham (1,516)
Field & Staff Officers: 1
57th Pennsylvania – Col. Peter Sides (207)
63rd Pennsylvania – Maj. John A. Dank (246)
68th Pennsylvania – Col. Andrew H. Tippin (320)
105th Pennsylvania – Col. Calvin A. Craig (274)
114th Pennsylvania – Lt.Col. Frederick F. Cavada (259)
141st Pennsylvania – Col. Henry J. Madill (209)

2ND BRIGADE:
Brig.Gen. J. Hobart Ward (Col.Hiram Berdan) (2,187)
Field & Staff Officers: 6
3rd Maine – Col. Moses B. Lakeman (210)
4th Maine – Col. Elijah Walker (287)
1st US Sharpshooters – Col. Hiram Berdan (313)
2nd US Sharpshooters – Maj. Homer R. Stoughton (169)
86th New York – Lt.Col. Benjamin L. Higgins (286)
124th New York – Col. A. Van Horne Ellis (238)
20th Indiana – Col. John Wheeler (401)
99th Pennsylvania – Maj. John W. Moore (277)

3RD BRIGADE:
Col. P. Regis de Trobriand (1,387)
Field & Staff Officers: 1
3rd Michigan – Col. Byron R. Pierce (237)
5th Michigan – Lt.Col. John Pulford (216)
17th Maine – Col. Chas. B. Merrill (350)
40th New York – Col. Thomas W. Egan (431)
110th Pennsylvania – Lt.Col. David M. Jones (152)

2ND DIVISION

Brig.Gen. Andrew A. Humphreys (4,960)
Field & Staff Officers: 4

1ST BRIGADE:
Brig.Gen. Joseph B. Carr (1,718)
Field & Staff Officers: 2
1st Massachusetts – Lt.Col. Clark B. Baldwin (321)
11th Massachusetts – Lt.Col. Porter D. Tripp (286)
16th Massachusetts – Lt.Col. Waldo Merriman (245)
26th Pennsylvania – Maj. Robert L. Bodine (365)
84th Pennsylvania – Lt.Col. Milton Opp (guarding baggage)
11th New Jersey – Col. Robert McAllister (275)
12th New Hampshire – Capt. John F. Langley (224)

2ND BRIGADE:
Col.Wm. R. Brewster (1,842)
Field & Staff Officers: 3
70th New York – Col. J. Egbert Farnum (288)
71st New York – Col. Henry L. Potter (248)
72nd New York – Col. John S. Austin (305)
73rd New York – Maj. Michael W. Burns (349)

74th New York – Lt.Col. Thomas Holt (266)
120th New York – Lt.Col. Cornelius D. Westbrook (383)

3RD BRIGADE:
Col.George C. Burling (1,396)
Field & Staff Officers: 2
5th New Jersey – Col. Wm. J. Sewell (206)
6th New Jersey – Lt.Col. Stephen R. Gilkyson (207)
7th New Jersey – Col. Louis R. Francine (275)
8th New Jersey – Col. John Ramsey (170)
115th Pennsylvania – Maj. John P. Dunne (182)
2nd New Hampshire – Col. Edward L. Bailey (354)

III CORPS ARTILLERY BRIGADE
Capt. George E. Randolph (616)
Field & Staff Officers: 2
B/2nd N.J. – Capt. Judson A. Clarke (143) (6/10P)
E/1st Rhode Island – 1st Lt. John K. Bucklyn (108) (6/N)
K/4th US Arty – 1st Lt. Francis W. Seeley (121) (6/N)
D/1st New York Lt. Arty – Capt. George B. Winslow (116) (6/N)
4th New York Lt. Arty – Capt. James E. Smith (126) (6/10P)

V CORPS

Maj.Gen. George Sykes (10,997)
Field & Staff Officers: 7

General HQ Provost Guard: **Cos D/E 12th New York** – Capt. Henry W. Rider (109)
D and H/17th Pennsylvania Cavalry – Capt. Wm. Thompson (78)

1ST DIVISION

Brig.Gen. James Barnes (3,420)
Field & Staff Officers: 4

1ST BRIGADE:
Col. Wm. S. Tilton (655)
Field & Staff Officers: 1
18th Massachusetts – Col. Joseph Hayes (139)
22nd Massachusetts – Lt.Col. Thomas Sherwin Jr. (137)
1st Michigan – Col. Ira C. Abbott (145)
118th Pennsylvania – Lt.Col. James Gwynn (233)

2ND BRIGADE:
Col. Jacob B. Sweitzer (1,423)
Field & Staff Officers: 1
9th Massachusetts – Col. Patrick R. Gwiney (412)
32nd Massachusetts – Col. G.L. Prescott (242)
4th Michigan – Col. Harrison H. Jeffords (342)
62nd Pennsylvania – Lt.Col. James C. Hull (426)

3RD BRIGADE:
Col. Strong Vincent (1,336)
Field & Staff Officers: 1
20th Maine – Col. Joshua L. Chamberlain (386)
44th New York – Col. James R. Rice (391)
83rd Pennsylvania – Capt. Orpheus S. Woodward (295)
16th Michigan – Col. Norwal E. Welch (263)

2ND DIVISION

Brig.Gen. Romeyn B. Ayres (4,002)
Field & Staff Officers: 5

1ST BRIGADE:
Col. Hannibal Day (1,553)
Field & Staff Officers: 2
3rd US Inf. – Capt. Henry W. Freedling (300)
4th US Inf. – Capt. Julius W. Adams Jr. (173)
6th US Inf. – Capt. Levi C. Bootes (150)
12th US Inf. – Capt. Thomas S. Dunne (415)
14th US Inf. – Maj. Grotius R. Giddings (513)

2ND BRIGADE:
Col. S. Burbank (953)
Field & Staff Officers: 1
2nd US INf. – Maj. Arthur T. Lee (197)
7th US INf. – Capt. David P. Hancock (116)
10th US Inf. – Capt. Wm. Clinton (93)
11th US Inf. – Maj. DeLancey Floyd-Jones (286)
17th US Inf. – Lt.Col. J. Durrell Greene (260)

3RD BRIGADE:
Brig.Gen. S.H. Weed (1,491)
Field & Staff Officers: 4
140th New York – Col. Patrick H. O'Rorke (449)
146th New York – Col. Kenner Garrard (456)
91st Pennsylvania – Lt.Col. Joseph Sinex (220)
155th Pennsylvania – Lt.Col. John H. Cain (362)

3RD DIVISION

Brig.Gen. Samuel W. Crawford (2,949)
Field & Staff Officers: 5

1ST BRIGADE:
Col. Wm. McCandless (1,235)
Field & Staff Officers: 1
1st Pennsylvania Reserves – Col. Wm. C. Talley (379)
2nd Pennsylvania reserves – Lt.Col. George A. Woodward (233)
6th Pennsylvania Reserves – Lt.Col. Wellington H. Ent (324)
13th Pennsylvania Reserves – Col. Chas. F. Taylor (298)

***2ND BRIGADE:**
Not transferred, left in Dept. of Washington

3RD BRIGADE:
Col. Joseph W. Fisher (1,709)
Field & Staff Officers: 1
5th Pennsylvania Reserves – Lt.Col. George Dare (285)
9th Pennsylvania Reserves – Lt.Col. James Mck. Snodgrass (322)
10th Pennsylvania Reserves – Col. Adoniram J. Warner (401)
11th Pennsylvania Reserves – Col. Samuel M. Jackson (327)
12th Pennsylvania Reserves – Col. Martin D. Hardin (373)

V CORPS ARTILLERY BRIGADE
Capt. Augustus P. Martin (432)
Field & Staff Officers: 3
D/5th US Arty – 1st Lt. Chas. Hazlett (68) (6/10P)
I/5th US Arty – 1st Lt. Malbone F. Watson (71) (4/3R)
C/1st New York – Capt. Almont Barnes (62) (4/3R)

L/1st Ohio – Capt. Frank C. Gibbs (113) (6/N)
C/3rd Mass. Lt. Arty – 1st Lt. Aaron F. Walcott (115) (6/N)

VI CORPS

Maj.Gen. J. Sedgewick (13,917)

HQ: **L/1st New Jersey Cavalry** (54) and H/1st Pennsylvania Cavalry (32) – Capt. Wm. S. Craft (86)
1st Massachusetts Cavalry (temporarily attached) – Lt.Col. Greely Stevenson Curtis (250)

1ST DIVISION

Brig.Gen. H.G. Wright (4,199)
Provost Guard: **A/C/H 4th New Jersey** – Maj. Charles Ewing (80)
Field & Staff Officers: 13

1ST BRIGADE:

Brig.Gen. A. Torbert (1,304)
Field & Staff Officers: 6
1st New Jersey – Lt.Col. Wm. Henry Jr. (253)
2nd New Jersey – Lt.Col. Chas. Wiebecke (357)
3rd New Jersey – Lt.Col. Edward L. Campbell (282)
15th New Jersey – Col. Wm. H. Penrose (410)

2ND BRIGADE:

Brig.Gen. Joseph J. Bartlett (1,325)
Field & Staff Officers: 4
95th Pennsylvania – Lt.Col. Edward Carroll (309)
96th Pennsylvania – Maj. Wm. H. Lessig (309)
5th Maine – Col. Clark S. Edwards (293)
121st New York – Col. Emory Upton (410)

3RD BRIGADE:

Brig.Gen. David A. Russell (1,484)
Field & Staff Officers: 6
49th Pennsylvania – Lt.Col. Thomas M. Hulings (276)
119th Pennsylvania – Col. Peter C. Ellmaker (404)
6th Maine – Col. Hiram Burnham (378)
5th Wisconsin – Col. Thomas S. Allen (420)

2ND DIVISION

Brig.Gen. Albion P. Howe (3,666)
Field & Staff Officers: 3

1ST BRIGADE:

NO FIRST BRIGADE IN DIVISION

2ND BRIGADE:

Col. Lewis A. Grant (1,888)
Field & Staff Officers/Band: 16
2nd Vermont – Col. Thomas H. Walbridge (444)
3rd Vermont – Col. Thomas O. Seaver (365)
4th Vermont – Col. Chas. B. Stoughton (437)
5th Vermont – Lt.Col. John R. Lewis (295)
6th Vermont – Col. Elisha L. Barney (331)

3RD BRIGADE:

Brig.Gen. Thomas H. Neill (1,775)
Field & Staff Officers/Band: 16
33rd New York – Capt. Henry J. Gifford (60)
43rd New York – Lt.Col. John Wilson (370)
49th New York – Col. Daniel B. Bidwell (359)
77th New York – Lt.Col. Winsor B. French (368)
61st Pennsylvania – Lt.Col. George F. Smith (386)
7th Maine – Lt.Col. Seldon Connor (216)

3RD DIVISION

Maj.Gen. John Newton (Brig.Gen. Frank Wheaton) (4,768)
Field & Staff Officers: 6

1ST BRIGADE:

Brig.Gen. Alexander Shaler (1,770)
Field & Staff Officers: 3
65th New York – Col. Joseph E. Hamblin (277)
67th New York – Col. Nelson Cross (349)
122nd New York – Col. Silus Titus (396)
23rd Pennsylvania – Lt.Col. John F. Glenn (437)
82nd Pennsylvania – Col. Isaac C. Bassett (278)

2ND BRIGADE:

Col. Henry L. Eustis (1,623)
Field & Staff Officers: 1
7th Massachusetts – Lt.Col. Franklin P. Harlow (320)
10th Massachusetts – Lt.Col. Joseph B. Parson (361)
37th Massachusetts – Col. Oliver Edwards (593)
2nd Rhode Island – Col. Horatio Rogers Jr. (348)

3RD BRIGADE:

Col. David J. Nevin (1,369)
Field & Staff Officers: 1
93rd Pennsylvania – Maj. John R. Nevin (234)
98th Pennsylvania – Maj. John B. Kohler (351)
102nd Pennsylvania – Col. John W. Patterson (guarding baggage);(103 went into battle w/wagons July 3rd, 1863)
139th Pennsylvania – Col. Frederick H. Collier (443)
62nd New York – Lt.Col. Theodore B. Hamilton (237)

VI CORPS ARTILLERY BRIGADE

Col. Chas. H. Tompkins (935)
Field & Staff Officers: 3
D/2nd US Arty – 1st Lt. Edward B. Williston (112) (6/N)
G/2nd US Arty – 1st Lt. John H. Butler (113) (6/N)
C/1st Rhode Island – Capt. Richard Waterman (116) (6/3R)
G/1st Rhode Island – Capt. George H. Adams (126) (6/10P)
1st Btty New York Light – Capt. Andrew Cowan (103) (6/3R)
3rd Btty New York Light – Capt. Wm. A. Harn (111) (6/10P)
A/1st Massachusetts Light – Capt. Wm. H. McCartney (135) (6/N)
F/5th US Arty – 1st Lt. Leonard Martin (116) (6/10P)

XI CORPS

Maj.Gen. Oliver Otis Howard (9,226)
Field & Staff Officers: 11

HQ: I&K/1st Indiana Cavalry – Capt. Abraham Sharra (52)
8th New York Inf. – 1st Lt. Hermann Foerster (40)
K/17th Pennsylvania Cavalry – Col. Josiah H. Kellogg (36)

1ST DIVISION

Brig.Gen. F. C. Barlow (Brig.Gen. Aldelbert Ames) (2,477)
Field & Staff Officers: 4

1ST BRIGADE:
Col. Leopold von Gilsa (1,136)
Field & Staff Officers: 2
41st New York – Lt.Col. Detleo von Einsiedel (218)
54th New York – Maj. Steven Kovaks (189)
68th New York – Col. Gotthilf Bourry (230)
153rd Pennsylvania – Maj. John J. Freuhauff (497)

2ND BRIGADE:
Brig.Gen. Aldelbert Ames (1,337)
Field & Staff Officers: 4
25th Ohio – Lt.Col. Jeremiah Williams (220)
75th Ohio – Col. Andrew L. Harris (269)
107th Ohio – Col. Seraphim Meyer (458)
17th Connecticut – Lt.Col. Douglas Fowler (386)

2ND DIVISION

Brig.Gen. Adolph von Steinwehr (2,897)
Field & Staff Officers: 5

Provost Guard: **29 New York** – 2nd Lt. Hans von Brandis (36)

1ST BRIGADE:
Col. Chas. R. Coster (1,217)
Field & Staff Officers: 5
27th Pennsylvania – Lt.Col. Lorenz Cantador (283)
73rd Pennsylvania – Capt. Daniel F. Kelly (290)
134th New York – Lt.Col. Allen H. Jackson (400)
154th New York – Lt.Col. Daniel B. Allen (239)

2ND BRIGADE:
Col. Orland Smith (1,639)
Field & Staff Officers: 1
55th Ohio – Col. Chas. B. Gambee (327)
73rd Ohio – Lt.Col. Richard Long (338)
33rd Massachusetts – Col. Aden B. Underwood (491)
136th New York – Col. James Wood Jr. (482)

3RD DIVISION

Maj.Gen. Carl Schurz (3,109)
Field & Staff Officers: 6

1ST BRIGADE:
Brig.Gen. Alexander von Schimmelfennig (1,683)
Field & Staff Officers: 3
45th New York – Lt.Col. Adolphus Dobke (375)
157th New York – Col. Philip S. Brown (409)
74th Pennsylvania – Col. Adolph von Hartung (333)
61st Ohio – Col. Steven J. McGroaty (247)
82nd Illinois – Lt.Col. Edward Salmon (316)

2ND BRIGADE:
Col. Wladimir Kryzanowski (1,420)
Field & Staff Officers: 3
58th New York – Lt.Col. August Otto (194)
119th New York – Col. John T. Lockman (262)
75th Pennsylvania – Col. Francis Mahler (208)
82nd Ohio – Col. James S. Robinson (312)
26th Wisconsin – Lt.Col. Hans Boebel (443)

XI CORPS ARTILLERY BRIGADE
Maj. Thomas W. Osborne (604)
Field & Staff Officers: 1
I/1st Ohio – Capt. Hubert Dilger (127) (6/N)
K/1st Ohio – Capt. Lewis Hickman (110) (4/N)
I/1st New York – Capt. Michael Wiedrick (141) (6/3R)
G/4th US Arty – 1st Lt. Bayard Wilkeson (115) (6/N)
13th New York – 1st Lt. Wm. Wheeler (110) (4/3R)

XII CORPS

Maj.Gen. H.W. Slocum (Maj.Gen. Alpheus S. Williams) (9,983)
Field & Staff Officers: 5

HQ Provost Guard: **Battalion/10th Maine** – Capt. John D. Beardsley (170)
D/H 9th New York Cavalry – Col. Wm. Sackett (75)

1ST DIVISION

Maj.Gen. Alpheus S. Williams (Brig.Gen. Thomas H. Ruger) (5,357)
Field & Staff Officers: 5

1ST BRIGADE:
Col. Archibald McDougall (1,836)
Field & Staff Officers: 1
5th Connecticut – Col. W.W. Packer (221)
20th Connecticut – Lt.Col. Wm. B. Wooster (321)
123rd New York – Lt.Col. James C. Rogers (495)
145th New York – Col. E.L. Price (245)
46th Pennsylvania – Col. James L. Selfridge (262)
3rd Maryland – Col. Joseph M. Sudsburg (290)

2ND BRIGADE:
Brig.Gen. Henry H. Lockwood (not assigned until after battle as part of 1st Division) (1,934)
Field & Staff Officers: 3
150th New York – Col. John H. Ketcham (609)
1st Maryland (Potomac Home Bde.) – Col. Wm. P. Maulsby (739)
1st Maryland (Eastern Shore) – Col. James Wallace (583)

3RD BRIGADE:
Brig.Gen. Thomas H. Ruger (Col. Silas Cosgrove) (1,582)
Field & Staff Officers: 1
2nd Massachusetts – Lt.Col. Chas. R. Mudge (316)
107th New York – Col. Niron M. Crane (319)
13th NJ – Col. Ezra A. Carman (347)
3rd Wisconsin – Col. Wm. Hawley (260)
27th Indiana – Col. Silas Cosgrove (339)

2ND DIVISION

Brig.Gen. John W. Geary (3982)
Field & Staff Officers: 5

Provost Guard: **B/28th Pennsylvania** – Capt. John Hornbuckle Flynn (27)

1ST BRIGADE:
Col. Chas. Candy (1,816)
Field & Staff Officers/Band: 17
5th Ohio – Col. John H. Patrick (302)
7th Ohio – Col. Wm. R. Creighton (282)
29th Ohio – Capt. Wilbur F. Stevens (308)
66th Ohio – Lt.Col. Eugene Powell (303)

28th Pennsylvania – Capt. John Flynn (306)
147th Pennsylvania – Lt.Col. Ario Pardee Jr. (298)

2ND BRIGADE:
Brig.Gen. Thomas L. Kane (Col. George A. Cobham) (700)
Field & Staff Officers: 3
29th Pennsylvania – Col. Wm. Richards Jr. (357)
109th Pennsylvania – Capt. F.L. Gimber (149)
111th Pennsylvania – Lt.Col. Thomas M. Walker (191)

3RD BRIGADE:
Brig.Gen. G.S. Green (1,424)
Field & Staff Officers: 3
60th New York – Col. Abel Godard (273)
78th New York – Lt.Col. Herbert von Hammerstein (198)
102nd New York – Col. James C. Lane (230)
137th New York – Col. David Ireland (423)
149th New York – Col. Henry A. Barnum (297)

XII CORPS ARTILLERY BRIGADE
1st Lt. E. D. Muhlenberg (391)
Field & Staff Officers: 1
F/4th US Arty – 1st Lt. Sylvanus T. Rugg (89) (6/N)
K/5th US Arty – 1st Lt. David H. Kinzie (72) (4/N)
M/1st New York Light Btty – 1st Lt. Charles E. Winegar (90) (4/10P)
E/Knap's Pennsylvania Light Btty – 1st Lt. Chas. A. Atwell (139) (6/10P)

CAVALRY CORPS

Maj.Gen. Alfred A. Pleasonton (11,475)
Field & Staff Officers: 24
General HQ: **I/1st Maine Cavalry** – Lt.Col. Chas. H. Smith (30)

1ST DIVISION

Brig.Gen. John Buford (4,239)
Field & Staff Officers: 4

1ST BRIGADE:
Col. Wm. Gamble (1612)
Field & Staff Officers: 4
8th New York – Lt.Col. Wm. L. Markell (580)
8th Illinois – Maj. John L. Beveridge (470)
2 sqdns/12th Illinois and 3 sqdns/3rd Indiana – Col. George H. Chapman (233+313=558 total)

2ND BRIGADE:
Col. Thomas C. Devin (1,113)
Field & Staff Officers: 5
6th New York – Maj. Wm. Beardsley (218)
3rd West Virginia – Capt. Seymour B. Conger (59)
9th New York – Col. Wm. E. Sackett (367)
17th Pennsylvania – Col. Josiah H. Kellogg (464)

RESERVE BRIGADE:
Brig.Gen. Wesley Merritt (1321)
Field & Staff Officers: 4
1st US Cavalry – -Capt. Richard S.C. Lord (362)
2nd US Cavalry – Capt. T. F. Rodenbaugh (407)
5th US Cavalry – Capt. Julius W. Mason (306)
6th US Cavalry – Maj. Samuel H. Starr (not at Gettysburg battlefield)
6th Pennsylvania – Maj. James H. Haseltine (242)

1ST DIVISION ARTILLERY

A/2nd (Tidball's) US Arty – Lt. John H. Calef (75) (6/3R)
K/1st US Arty – Capt. Wm. M. Graham (114) (6/3R)

2ND DIVISION

Brig.Gen. David McM. Gregg (2,639)
HQ Guard: **C/1st Ohio Cavalry** – Capt. Samuel N. Stanford (44)

1ST BRIGADE:
Col. John B. McIntosh (1,248)
Field & Staff Officers/Band: 19
1st New Jersey – Maj. M. H. Beaumont (199)
H/3rd Pennsylvania Hvy Arty (as Light) – Capt. W.D. Rank (52)
3rd Pennsylvania – Lt.Col. E.S. Jones (335)
A/Purnell Maryland Legion – Capt. Robert E. Duvall (66)
1st Maryland – Lt.Col. James M. Deems (285)
1st Massachusetts – Lt.Col. Greeley S. Curtis (served w/VI Corps on rt. flank) (292)

2ND BRIGADE:
Col. Pinnock Huey (Westminster, not in battle) (1,436)
Field & Staff Officers: 1
2nd New York – Lt.Col. Otto Harhaus (264)
4th New York – Lt.Col. Augustus Pruyn (298)
8th Pennsylvania – Capt. Wm. A. Corrie (39[illegible])
6th Ohio – Maj. Wm. Stedman (482)

3RD BRIGADE:
Col. J. Irvin Gregg (1,347)
Field & Staff Officers: 8
4th Pennsylvania – Lt.Col. Wm. E. Doster (258)
16th Pennsylvania – Lt.Col. John K. Robison (349)
10th New York – Maj. M. Henry Avery (333)
1st Maine – Lt.Col. Chas. H. Smith (315)
2nd Division Artillery E/G 1st US Arty – Capt. Alanson M Randol (84) (4/3R)

3RD DIVISION

Brig.Gen. Judson Kilpatrick (4081)
Field & Staff Officers: 3

HQ Guard: **A/1st Ohio** – Capt. Noah Jones (41)

1ST BRIGADE:
Brig.Gen. Elon J. Farnsworth (1,925)
Field & Staff Officers: 1
5th New York – Maj. John Hammond (420)
18th Pennsylvania – Lt.Col. Wm. P. Brinton (509)
1st Vermont – Lt.Col. Addison W. Preston (600)
1st West Virginia – Col. Nathaniel P. Richmond (395)

2ND BRIGADE:
Brig.Gen. George Armstrong Custer (1,934)
Field & Staff Officers: 1
1st Michigan – Col. Chas. H. Town (427)
5th Michigan – Col. Russell A. Alger (646)
6th Michigan – Col. George Gray (477)
7th Michigan – Col. Wm. D. Mann (383)

3RD DIVISION ARTILLERY (178)

M/2nd US Arty – 1st Lt. A.C.M. Pennington Jr. (117) (6/3R)
E/4th US Arty – 1st Lt. Samuel Elder (61) (4/3R)
Horse Artillery Cavalry Reserve Artillery (459)

1ST BRIGADE:
Capt. James M. Robertson (315)
Field & Staff Officers: 2
B & L/2nd US Arty – 1st Lt. Edward Heaton (99) (6/3R)
6th New York Btty – Capt. Joseph W. Martin (103) (6/3R)
9th Michigan Btty – Capt. Jabez J. Daniels (111) (6/3R)

2ND BRIGADE:
Capt. John C. Ticball (144)
Field & Staff Officers: 2
(Parts serving with 1st Division)
C/3rd US Arty – 1st Lt. Wm. D. Fuller (w/Huey's cavalry, not in battle) (142)

ARTILLERY RESERVE

Brig.Gen. Robert O. Tyler (2619)
Field & Staff Officers: 46
Ordnance Detachment – 11

HQ Guard: **C/32nd Massachusetts** – Col. George L. Prescott (45)
Guard Ammunition Train – **BDEFGIK/4th NJ** – Maj. Charles Ewing (273)

1ST REGULAR BRIGADE:
Capt. Dunbar R. Ransom (445)
Field & Staff Officers: 2
H/1st US Arty – 1st Lt. Chandler P. Eakin (129) (6/N)
F & K/3rd US Arty – 1st Lt. John G. Turnbull (115) (6/N)
C/4th US Arty – 1st Lt. Evan Thomas (95) (6/N)
C/5th US Arty – 1st Lt. Gulian V. Wier (104) (6/N)

1ST VOLUNTEER BRIGADE:
Lt.Col. Freeman McGilvery (391)
Field & Staff Officers: 2
5th Massachusetts Light (10th New York attached) – Capt. Chas. A. Phillips (104) (6/3R)
9th Massachusetts Light – Capt. John Bigelow (110) (6/N)
15th New York Light – Capt. Patrick Hart (70) (4/N)
C & F/Pennsylvania Lt. Independent Btty – Capt. James Thompson (105) (6/3R)

2ND VOLUNTEER BRIGADE:
Capt. Elijah D. Taft (477)
Field & Staff Officers: 2
B/1st Connecticut Heavy – Capt. Albert F. Brooker (110) (4/4.5R) (At Westminster)
M/1st Connecticut Heavy – Capt. Franklin A. Pratt (110)
2nd Connecticut Light – Capt. John W. Sterling (109) (4/JR, 2/12H)
5th New York Light – Capt. Elijah D. Taft (146) (6/20P)

3RD VOLUNTEER BRIGADE:
Capt. James F. Huntington (481)
Field & Staff Officers: 2
F & G/1st Pennsylvania – Capt. R. Bruce Ricketts (144) (6/3R)
H/1st Ohio – 1st Lt. George W. Norton (99) (6/3R)
A/1st New Hampshire Light – Capt. Frederick M Edgell (86) (4/3R)
C/1st West Virginia-Capt. Wallace Hill (100) (4/10P)

4TH VOLUNTEER BRIGADE:
Capt. Robert H. Fitzhugh (500)
Field & Staff Officers: 2
G/1st New York Light – Capt. Nelson Ames (84) (6/N)
K/1st New York Light – Capt. Robert H. Fitzhugh (122) (6/3R)
A/1st Maryland Light – Capt. James H. Rigby (107) (6/3R)

F/6th Maine Light – 1st Lt. Edwin B. Dow (87) (4/N)
A/1st New Jersey Light – 1st Lt. Augustin N. Parsons (98) (6/10P)

Confederates started the war dressed in regulation uniforms, but at Gettysburg most Southerners wore butternut or ragged original-issue clothing.

ARMY OF NORTHERN VIRGINIA

Gen. Robert E. Lee
(75,000 total; 69,700 engaged)
Field & Staff Officers: 17
A/C 39th Virginia Cav. Battalion – Maj. John H. Richardson (91)

I CORPS

Lt.Gen. James Longstreet (21,031)
Field & Staff Officers: 16

1ST DIVISION

Maj.Gen. Lafayette McLaws (7,138)

1ST BRIGADE (KERSHAW'S BRIGADE):
Brig.Gen. J.B. Kershaw (2,183)
Field & Staff Officers: 6
2nd South Carolina – Col. J.D. Kennedy (412)
3rd South Carolina – Maj. R. C. Maffett (406)
7th South Carolina – Col. D. Wyatt Aiken (408)
8th South Carolina – Col. J.W. Henagan (300)
15th South Carolina – Col. W. D. de Saussure (448)
3rd South Carolina Battalion – Lt.Col. W. G. Rice (203)

2ND BRIGADE (BARKSDALE'S BRIGADE):
Brig.Gen. Wm. Barksdale (1,620)
Field & Staff Officers: 4
13th Mississippi – Col. J. W. Carter (481)
17th Mississippi – Col. W.D. Holder (469)
18th Mississippi – Col. T.M. Griffin (242)
21st Mississippi – Col. B.G. Humphreys (424)

3RD BRIGADE (SEMMES' BRIGADE):
Brig.Gen. P.J. Semmes (1,334)
Field & Staff Officers: 4
10th Georgia – Col. John B. Weems (303)
50th Georgia – Col. W.R. Manning (302)
51st Georgia – Col. E. Ball (303)
53rd Georgia – Col. James P. Simms (422)

4TH BRIGADE (WOFFORD'S BRIGADE):
Brig.Gen. W.T. Wofford (1,607)
Field & Staff Officers: 4
16th Georgia – Col. Goode Bryan (303)
18th Georgia – Lt.Col. S.Z. Ruff (302)
24th Georgia – Col. Robert McMillan (303)
Phillips Georgia Legion – Lt.Col. E.S. Barclay (273)
Cobb's Georgia Legion – Lt.Col. Luther J. Glenn (213)
3rd Batallion Georgia Sharpshooters – (209)

1ST DIVISION ARTILLERY BRIGADE
Col. H. G. Cabell (378)
Field & Staff Officers: 4
A/1st North Carolina – Capt. B.C. Manley (131) (2/N, 2/3R)
1st Richmond Howitzers – Capt. E.S. McCarthy (90) (2/N,2/3R)
Pulaski Georgia Arty – Capt. J.C. Fraser (63) (2/3R,2/10P)
Troup Georgia Arty – Capt. H. H. Carlton (90) 2/12H,2/10P)

2ND DIVISION (PICKETT'S DIVISION)

Maj.Gen. George E. Pickett (5,580)
Field & Staff Officers: 11

1ST BRIGADE (GARNETT'S BRIGADE):
Brig.Gen. R.B. Garnett (1,459)
Field & Staff Officers: 4
8th Virginia – Col. Eppa Hunton (193)
18th Virginia – Lt.Col. A. Carrington (312)
19th Virginia – Col. Henry Gantt (328)
28th Virginia – Col. R.C. Allen (333)
56th Virginia – Col. W.D. Sturat (289)

2ND BRIGADE (KEMPER'S BRIGADE):
Brig.Gen. J. L. Kemper (1,741)
Field & Staff Officers: 11
1st Virginia – Col. Lewis B. Williams (209)
3rd Virginia – Col. Joseph Mayo Jr. (332)
7th Virginia – Col. W. T. Patton (335)
11th Virginia – Maj. Kirkwood Otey (359)
24th Virginia – Col. Wm. R. Terry (495)

3RD BRIGADE (ARMISTEAD'S BRIGADE):
Brig.Gen. L. A. Armistead (1,950)
Field & Staff Officers: 4
9th Virginia – Maj. John C. Ownes (257)
14th Virginia – Col. James G. Hodges (422)
38th Virginia – Col. E. C. Edmonds (356)
53rd Virginia – Col. W. R. Aylett (435)
57th Virginia – Col. John Bowie Magruder (476)

2ND DIVISION ARTILLERY BRIGADE
Maj. James Dearing (419)
Field & Staff Officers: 9
Fauquier Va. Arty – Capt. R.M. Stribling (134) (4/N,2/10P)
Hampden Va. Arty – Capt. W. H. Caskie (90) (2/N,1/10P,1/3R)
Richmond Fayette Arty – Capt. M.C. Macon (90) (2/N, 2/10P)
Virginia Btty – Capt. Joseph G. Blount (96) (4/N)

3RD DIVISION

Maj.Gen. John B. Hood (7,374)
Field & Staff Officers: 11

1ST BRIGADE (LAW'S BRIGADE):
Brig.Gen. E. M. Law (1,933)
Field & Staff Officers: 4
4th Alabama – Lt.Col. L. H. Scruggs (346)
15th Alabama – Col. Wm. C. Oates (499)
44th Alabama – Col. Wm. F. Perry (363)
47th Alabama – Col. James W. Jackson (347)
48th Alabama – Col. James L. Sheffield (374)

2ND BRIGADE (ANDERSON'S BRIGADE):
Brig.Gen. George T. Anderson (1,874)
Field & Staff Officers: 10
7th Georgia – Col. W.W. White (377)
8th Georgia – Col. John R. Towers (312)

9th Georgia – Lt Col. John C. Mounger (340)
11th Georgia – Col. F.H. Little (310)
59th Georgia – Col. Jack Brown (525)

3RD BRIGADE (ROBERTSON'S BRIGADE):
Brig.Gen. J.B. Robertson (1,734)
Field & Staff Officers: 5
1st Texas – Lt.Col. P.A. Work (426)
4th Texas – Col. J.C.G. Key (415)
5th Texas – Col. R.M. Powell (409)
3rd Arkansas – Col. Van H. Manning (479)

4TH BRIGADE (BENNING'S BRIGADE):
Brig.Gen. Henry L. Benning (1,419)
Field & Staff Officers: 4
2nd Georgia – Lt.Col. Wm. T. Harris (348)
15th Georgia – Col. D. M. DuBose (368)
17th Georgia – Col. W.C. Hodges (350)
20th Georgia – Col. John A. Jones (349)

3RD DIVISION ARTILLERY

Maj. W.M. Henry (403)
Field & Staff Officers: 9

F/13th (Branch) N.C. Arty – Capt. A.C. Latham (112) (1/6G, 1/12H,3/N)
D/1st (Rowan) N.C. Arty – Capt. James Reilly (148) (2/N,2/3R,2/10P)
Charleston (German) S.C. Lt. Arty – Capt. Wm. K. Bachman (71) (4/N)
Palmetto S.C. Light Arty – Capt. Hugh R. Garden (63) (2/N, 2/10P)

I CORPS ARTILLERY RESERVE BRIGADE
Col. J.B. Walton (923)
Field & Staff Officers: 4

Alexander's Battalion (581)
Field & Staff Oficers: 9
Ashland Va. Arty – Capt. P. Woolfolk Jr. (103) (4/N,2/20P)
Bedford Va. Arty – Capt. T.C. Jordan (78) (4/3R)
Brooks S.C. Arty – Lt. S.C. Gilbert (71) (4/12H)
Madison Louisiana Light Arty – Capt. George V. Moody (135) (4/24H)
Richmond, Virginia Btty – Capt. W. W. Parker (90) (3/3R,1/10P)
Bath, Virginia Btty – Capt. O.B. Taylor (95) (4/N)

Washington Louisiana Artillery Battalion (338)
Field & Staff Officers: 9
1st Company – Capt. C.B. Squires (77) (1/N)
2nd Company – Capt. J.B. Richardson (80) (2/N,1/12H)
3rd Company – Capt. M.B. Miller (92) (3/N)
4th Company – Capt. Joe Norcom (80) (2/N, 1/12H)

II ARMY CORPS

Lt.Gen. Richard S. Ewell (20,8664)
Field & Staff Officers: 14

HQ Escort: **Randolph's Company Virginia Cavalry** – Capt. Wm. F. Randolph (31)
A&B/**1st N.C. Bttn Sharpshooters Provost Guard** – Maj. Rufus W. Norton (94)

1ST DIVISION (EARLY'S DIVISION)

Maj.Gen. Jubal A. Early (5,458)
Field & Staff Officers: 12

1ST BRIGADE (HAYS' BRIGADE):
Brig.Gen. Harry T. Hays (1,295)
Field & Staff Officers: 3
5th Louisiana – Maj. Alexander Hart (196)
6th Louisiana – Lt.Col. Joseph Hanlon (218)
7th Louisisana – Col. D.B. Penn (235)
8th Louisiana – Col. T. D. Lewis (296)
9th Louisiana – Col. Leroy A. Stafford (347)

2ND BRIGADE (HOKE'S BRIGADE):
Col. Isaac E. Avery (1,244)
Field & Staff Officers: 2
6th North Carolina – Maj. S. McD. Tate (509)
21st North Carolina – Col. W.W. Kirkland (436)
57th North Carolina – Col. A.C. Godwin (297)

3RD BRIGADE (SMITH'S BRIGADE):
Brig.Gen. Wm. Smith (806)
Field & Staff Officers: 4
31st Virginia – Col. John S. Hoffman (267)
49th Virginia – Lt.Col. J. Catlett Gibson (281)
52nd Virginia – Lt.Col. James H. Skinner (254)

4TH BRIGADE (GORDON'S BRIGADE):
Brig.Gen. J.B. Gordon (1,508)
Field & Staff Officers: 6
13th Georgia – Col. James M. Smith (312)
31st Georgia – Col. Clement A. Evans (252)
38th Georgia – Capt. Wm. D. McLeod (341)
60th Georgia – Capt. W. B. Jones (299)
61st Georgia – Col. John H. Lamar (298)

1ST DIVISION ARTILLERY BRIGADE
Lt.Col. H.P. Jones (605)
Field & Staff Officers: 9
26th Georgia – Col. E.N. Atkinson (det. from 4th Bde.) (315)
Charlottesville Va. Arty – Capt. James McD. Carrington (71) (4/N)
Courtney Va. Arty – Capt. W.A. Turner (90) (4/3R)
Staunton Va. Arty – Capt. A. W. Garber (60) (4/N)
Louisiana Guard Arty – Capt. C.A. Green (60) (2/3R,2/10P)

2ND DIVISION (JOHNSON'S DIVISION)

Maj.Gen. Edward Johnson (6,380)
Field & Staff Officers: 9

1ST BRIGADE (STEUART'S BRIGADE):
Brig.Gen. George H. Steuart (212)
Field & Staff Officers: 5
1st Maryland Battalion Inf. – Lt.Col. J.R. Herbert (400)
1st North Carolina – Lt.Col. H.A. Brown (377)
3rd North Carolina – Maj. W. M. Parsley (548)
10th Virginia – Col. E.T.H. Warren (276)
23rd Virginia – Lt.Col. S.T. Walton (251)
37th Virginia – Maj. H.C. Wood (264)

2ND BRIGADE (STONEWALL BRIGADE):
Brig.Gen. James A. Walker (1,323)
Field & Staff Officers: 4
2nd Virginia – Col. J.Q.A. Nadenbousch (333)
4th Virginia – Maj. Wm. Terry (257)
5th Virginia – Col. J.H.S. Frank (345)
27th Virginia – Lt.Col. D.M. Shriver (148)
33rd Virginia – Capt. J. B. Golladay (236)

3RD BRIGADE (NICHOLL'S BRIGADE):
Col. J.M. Williams (1,104)
Field & Staff Officers: 3
1st Louisiana – Capt. E.D. Willett (172)
2nd Louisiana – Lt.Col. R. E. Burke (236)
10th Louisiana – Maj. T.N. Powell (226)
14th Louisiana – Lt.Col. David Zable (281)
15th Louisiana – Maj. Andrew Brady (186)

4TH BRIGADE (JONES' BRIGADE):
Brig.Gen. John M. Jones (1,467)
Field & Staff Officers: 7
21st Virginia – Capt. W.P. Moseley (183)
42nd Virginia – Col. J. C. Higgenbotham (265)
44th Virginia – Lt.Col. R. W. Withers (227)
48th Virginia – Lt.Col. R.H. Dungan (265)
50th Virginia – Lt.Col. L.H.N. Salyer (240)
25th Virginia – Col. George A. Porterfield (280)

2ND DIVISION ARTILLERY

Maj. J.W. Latimer (356)
Field & Staff Officers: 9

1st Maryland Btty – Capt. W.F. Dement (90) (4/N)
Allegheny Virginia Btty – Capt. J.C. Carpenter (91) (2/N, 2/3R)
Chesapeake Maryland Btty – Capt. Wm. D. Brown (76) (4/10H)
Lee Virginia Btty – Capt. C.I. Raine (90) (1/3R,1/10P,2/20P)

3RD DIVISION (RODES' DIVISION)

Maj.Gen. R. E. Rodes (7,499)
Field & Staff Officers: 14

1ST BRIGADE (DANIELS BRIGADE):
Brig.Gen. Junius Daniel (2,065)
Field & Staff Officers: 4
32nd North Carolina – Col. E.C. Brabble (454)
43rd North Carolina – Col. T.S. Keenan (572)
45th North Carolina – Lt.Col. S.H. Boyd (460)
53rd North Carolina – Col. W.A. Owens (322)
2nd North Carolina Battalion – Lt.Col. H. L. Andrews (253)

2ND BRIGADE (DOLES' BRIGADE):
Brig.Gen. George Doles (1,323)
Field & Staff Officers: 4
4th Georgia – Lt.Col. D.R.E. Winn (341)
12th Georgia – Col. Edward Willis (327)
21st Georgia – Col. John T. Mercer (287)
44th Georgia – Col. S.P. Lumpkin (364)

3RD BRIGADE (IVERSON'S BRIGADE)
Brig.Gen. Alfred Iverson (1,382)
Field & Staff Officers: 4
5th North Carolina – Capt. Speight B. West (473)
12th North Carolina – Col. W.S. Davis (2[illegible]9)
20th North Carolina – Lt.Col. Nelson Slough (372)
23rd North Carolina – Col. D. H. Christie (314)

4TH BRIGADE (RAMSEUR'S BRIGADE):
Brig.Gen. S.D. Ramseur (1,029)
Field & Staff Officers: 4
2nd North Carolina – Maj. D.W. Hurtt (243)
4th North Carolina – Col. Bryan Grimes (196)
14th North Carolina – Col. R. Tyler Bennett (306)
30th North Carolina – Col. Francis Parker (278)

5TH BRIGADE (RODES BRIGADE):
Col. E.A. O'Neal (1,688)
Field & Staff Officers: 3
3rd Alabama – Col. A. C. Battle (350)
5th Alabama – Col. J. M. Hall (317)
6th Alabama – Col. J.N. Lightfoot (382)
12th Alabama – Col. S.B. Pickens (317)
26th Alabama – Lt.Col. John C. Goodgame (319)

3RD DIVISION ARTILLERY

Lt.Col. Thomas H. Carter (385)
Field & Staff Officers: 4

Jefferson Davis ALa. Arty – Capt. W.J. Reese (79) (4/3R)
King William Va. Arty – Capt. W.P. Carter (103) (2/N,2/10P)
Morris Va. Arty – Capt. R.C.M. Page (114) (4/N)
Orange Va. Arty – Capt. C.W. Fry (80) (2/3R, 2/10P)

II CORPS ARTILLERY RESERVE

Col. J. Thompson Brown (644)
Field & Staff Officers: 4
1st Virginia (Dance's Bn) Arty – Capt. Willis J. Dance (367)
Field & Staff Officers: 9

2nd Richmond Va. Howitzers – Capt. David Watson (64) (4/10P)
3rd Richmond Va. Howitzers – Capt. B.H. Smith Jr (62) (4/3R)
Powhatan Va. Arty – 1st Lt. John M. Cunningham (78) (4/3R)
Rockbridge Va. Arty – Capt. A. Graham (85) (4/20P)
Salem Va. Arty – 1st Lt. C.B. Griffin (69) (2/N, 2/3R)

Nelson's Battalion
Lt.Col. Wm. Nelson (273)
Field & Staff Officers: 9
Amherst Va. Arty – Capt. J.J. Kirkpatrick (105) (3/N, 1/3R)
Fluvanna Va. Arty – Capt. J.L. Massie (90) (3/N, 1/3R)
Georgia Btty – Capt. John Milledge Jr. (69) (2/3R, 1/10P)

III ARMY CORPS

Lt.Gen. Ambrose P. Hill (26,793)
Field & Staff Officers: 15

1ST DIVISION (ANDERSON'S DIVISION)

Maj.Gen. R.H. Anderson (7,130)
Field & Staff Officers: 7

1ST BRIGADE (WILCOX'S BRIGADE):
Brig.Gen. Cadmus M. Wilcox (1,726)
Field & Staff Officers: 5
8th Alabama – Lt.Col. Hilary A. Herbert (477)
9th Alabama – Capt. J.H. King (306)
10th Alabama – Col. Wm. H. Forney (311)
11th Alabama – Col. J.C.C. Sanders (311)
14th Alabama – Col. L. Pinckard (316)

2ND BRIGADE – (MAHONE'S BRIGADE):
Brig.Gen. Wm. Mahone (1,542)
Field & Staff Officers: 4
6th Virginia – Col. George T. Rogers (288)
12th Virginia – Col. D.A. Weisener (348)
16th Virginia – Col. Joseph H. Ham (270)
41st Virginia – Col. Wm. A. Parham (276)
61st Virginia – Col. V.D. Grover (356)

3RD BRIGADE (WRIGHT'S BRIGADE)
Brig.Gen. A.R. Wright (1,413)
Field & Staff Officers: 4
3rd Georgia – Col. E.J. Walker (441)
22nd Georgia – Col. Joseph Wasden (400)
48th Georgia – Col. William Gibson (395)
2nd Georgia Battalion – Maj. George W. Rose (173)

4TH BRIGADE (PERRY'S BRIGADE):
Col. David Lang (742)
Field & Staff Officers: 3
2nd Florida – Maj. W.R. Moore (242)
5th Florida – Capt. R.N. Gardner (321)
8th Florida – Col. David Lang (176)

5TH BRIGADE (POSEY'S BRIGADE):
Brig.Gen. Carnot Posey (1,322)
Field & Staff Officers: 4
12th Mississippi – Col. W.H. Taylor (305)
16th Mississippi – Col. Samuel E. Baker (385)
19th Mississippi – Col. N.H. Harris (372)
48th Mississippi – Col. Joseph M Jayne (256)

1ST DIVISION ARTILLERY (SUMTER BATTALION)

Maj. John Lane (384)
Field & Staff Officers: 9

Co. A – Capt. Hugh Ross (130) (3/10P, 1/3NR, 1/12H, 1/N)
Co. B – Capt. George M. Patterson (124) (4/12H, 2/N)
Co. C – Capt John T. Wingfield (121) (3/3NR, 2/10P)

2ND DIVISION (HETH'S DIVISION)

Maj.Gen. Henry Heth (7,394)
Field & Staff Officers: 8

1ST BRIGADE (PETTIGREW'S BRIGADE):
Brig.Gen. J.J. Pettigrew (2,581)
Field & Staff Officers: 4
11th North Carolina – Col. Collett Leventhorpe (617)
26th North Carolina – Col. Henry K. Burgwyn Jr. (840)
47th North Carolina – Col. G. H. Faribault (567)
53rd North Carolina – Col. J.K. Marshall (553)

2ND BRIGADE (BROCKENBROUGH'S BRIGADE):
Col. J. M. Brockenbrough (971)
Field & Staff Officers: 4
40th Virginia – Capt. T.E. Betts (253)
47th Virginia – Col. Robert M. Mayo (209)
55th Virginia – Col. W.S. Christian (268)
22nd Virginia Battalion – Maj. John S. Bowles (237)

3RD BRIGADE (ARCHER'S BRIGADE):
Brig.Gen. James J. Archer (1197)
Field & Staff Officers: 4
13th Alabama – Col. B.D. Fry (308)
5th Alabama Battalion – Maj. A.S. Van de Graaff (135)
1st Tennessee Provisional Army – Maj. Felix G. Buchanan (281)
7th Tennessee – Lt.Col. S.G. Shepard (249)
14th Tennessee – Capt. B.L. Phillips (220)

4TH BRIGADE (DAVIS' BRIGADE):
Brig.Gen. Joseph R. Davis (2241)
Field & Staff Officers: 6
2nd Mississiipi – Col. J.M. Stone (492)
11th Mississippi – Col. F. M. Green (592)
42nd Mississippi – Col. H.R. Miller (511)
55th North Carolina – Col. J.K. Connally (640)

2ND DIVISION ARTILLERY

Lt.Col. John J. Garnett (396)
Field & Staff Officers: 9

Donaldsville Louisiana Arty – Capt. V. Maurin (114)
Huger Virgina Arty – Capt. Joseph D. Moore (77)
Lewis Virginia Arty – Capt. John W. Lewis (90)
Norfolk Light Arty Blues – Capt. C.R. Grandy (106)

3RD DIVISION (PENDER'S DIVISION)

Maj.Gen. Wm. D. Pender (6,681)
Field & Staff Officers: 11

1ST BRIGADE (PERRIN'S BRIGADE):
Col. Abner Perrin (1,882)
Field & Staff Officers: 4
1st South Carolina Rifles – Capt. Wm. D. Hadden (366)
1st South Carolina – Maj. C.W. McCreary (328)
12th South Carolina – Col. John L. Miller (366)
13th South Carolina – Lt.Col. B.T. Brockman (390)
14th South Carolina – Lt.Col. Joseph L. Brown (428)

2ND BRIGADE (LANE'S BRIGADE):
Brig.Gen. James H. Lane (1,734)
Field & Staff Officers: 4
7th North Carolina – Capt. J. McLeod Turner (291)
18th North Carolina – Col. John D. Barry (346)
28th North Carolina – Col. S.D. Lowe (346)
33rd North Carolina – Col. C. M. Avery (368)

French style Zouave and chasseur uniforms influenced the official clothing issue of both armies. In the field, both Union and Confederate soldiers dressed for comfort.

37th North Carolina – Col. W.M. Barbour (379)

3RD BRIGADE (THOMAS'S BRIGADE):
Brig.Gen. Edward L. Thomas (1,326)
Field & Staff Officers: 4
14th Georgia – Col. J.N. Brown (331)
35th Georgia – Capt. John Duke (331)
45th Georgia – Lt. W.L. Grice (331)
49th Georgia – Col. S.T. Player (329)

4TH BRIGADE (SCALES' BRIGADE):
Brig.Gen. A.M. Scales (1351)
Field & Staff Officers: 4
13th North Carolina – Col. J.H. Rogers (232)
16th North Carolina – Capt. L.W. Stowe (321)
22nd North Carolina – Col. James Conner (267)
34th North Carolina – Col. Wm. Lee J. Lowrance (311)
38th North Carolina – Col. W.J. Hoke (216)

3RD DIVISION ARTILLERY

Col. Wm. T. Poague (377)
Field & Staff Officers: 4

Albemarle Va. Arty – Capt. James W. Wyatt (94) (1/12H, 2/3R, 1/10P)
Charlotte North Carolina Arty – Capt. Joseph Graham (125) (2/12H, 2/N)
Madison Mississippi Light Arty – Capt. George Ward (91) (1/12H, 3/N)
Warrenton, Virginia Btty – Capt. J.V. Brooke (58) (2/12H, 2/N)

III CORPS

ARTILLERY RESERVE

Col. R. Lindsay Walker (722)
Field & Staff Officers: 4

McIntosh's Battalion – Maj. D.G. McIntosh
Danville Va. Arty – Capt. R.S. Rice (114) (4/N)
2nd Hardaway Alabama Arty – Capt. W.B. Hurt (71) (2/3R, 2W)
2nd Rockbridge Va. Arty (Luck's Btty) – 1st Lt. Samuel Wallace (67) (2/N, 2/3R)
Johnson's Richmond, Virginia Btty – Capt. M. Johnson (96) (4/3R)

Pegram's Battalion – Maj. W.J. Pegram (370)
Richmond (Crenshaw) Va. Btty – **[Johnston]** (76) (2/12H, 2/N)
Fredericksburg Va. Arty – Capt. E.A. Marye (75) (2/N, 2/3R)
Letcher Va. Arty – Capt. T.A. Brander (65) (2/N, 2/10R)
PeeDee South Carolina Arty – 1st Lt. Wm E. Zimmerman (65) (4/3R)
Richmond (Purcell) Va. Arty – Capt. Joseph McGraw (89) (4/N)

CAVALRY DIVISION

Maj.Gen. James Ewell Brown (JEB) Stuart (6,482)
Field & Staff Officers: 20

1ST BRIGADE (HAMPTON'S BRIGADE):
Brig.Gen. Wade Hampton (1751)
Field & Staff Officers: 5
1st North Carolina – Col. L.S. Barker (407)
1st South Carolina – Brig.Gen. Wade Hampton (339)
2nd South Carolina – Col. M.C. Butler (186)
Cobb's Georgia Legion – Col. P.B.M. Young (330)
Jefferson Davis Legion – Lt.Col. J.F. Warring (246)
Phillips Georgia Legion – Lt.Col. J.C. Phillips (238)

2ND BRIGADE (ROBERTSON'S BRIGADE):
Brig.Gen. Beverly H. Robertson (966)
Guarding right flank at Fairfield, not engaged at Gettysburg
Field & Staff Officers: 4
4th North Carolina – Col. D. D. Ferebee (504)
5th North Carolina – Col. Thomas M. Garrett (458)

3RD BRIGADE (JONES' BRIGADE):
Brig.Gen. Wm. E. Jones (1,713)
Guarding right flank at Fairfield, not engaged at Gettysburg.
Field & Staff Officers: 4
6th Virginia – Maj. C.E. Flournoy (625)
7th Virginia – Lt.Col. Thomas Marshall (428)
11th Virginia – Col. L.L. Lomax (424)

35th Va. Cavalry Battalion – Lt.Col. Elijah V. White (232)
At Gettysburg

4TH BRIGADE (FITZHUGH LEE'S BRIGADE):
Brig.Gen. Fitzhugh Lee (1,913)
Field & Staff Officers: 4
1st Maryland Battalion – Maj. Harry Gilmor (310)
1st Virginia – Col. James H. Drake (310)
2nd Virginia – Col. T.T. Munford (385)
3rd Virginia – Col. Thomas H. Owen (210)
4th Virginia – Col. Williams C. Wickham (544)
5th Virginia – Col. T.L. Rosser (150)

5TH BRIGADE (JENKINS BRIGADE):
Brig.Gen. A.G Jenkins (1,179)
Field & Staff Officers: 4
14th Virginia – Col. Charles E. Thoburn (265)
16th Virginia – Col. Milton J. Ferguson (265)
17th Virginia – Col. Wm. H. French (241)
34th Virginia Battalion – Lt.Col. V.A. Witcher (172)
36th Virginia Battalion – Col. M.J. Ferguson (125)
Charlottesville (Jackson's), Virginia Btty – Capt. Thomas E. Jackson (107)

6TH BRIGADE (W.H.F. LEE'S BRIGADE):
Col. J.R. Chambles (1,173)
Field & Staff Officers: 4
2nd North Carolina – Col. Samuel B. Spruill (145)
9th Virginia – Col. R.L.T. Beale (490)
10th Virginia – Col. J. Lucius Davis (236)
13th Virginia – Col. Jefferson C. Phillips (298)

Beckham's Battalion:
Maj. R.F. Beckham (434)
Field & Staff Officers: 9
1st Stuart's Horse Arty/Breathed's Virginia Btty – Capt. James Breathed (106) (4/3R)
Chew's Virginia Btty – Capt. R.P. Chew (99) (4 guns) w/Jones, not at Gettysburg
2nd Baltimore Griffin's Maryland Btty – Capt. W.H. Griffin (106) (4/10P)
Hart's South Carolina Btty – Capt. J.F. Hart (107) (8/BR)
2nd Stuart's Horse Arty/McGregor's Virginia Btty – Capt. W. M. McGregor (106) (2/N, 2/3R)
Moorman's Virginia Btty – Capt. M.N. Moorman (112) (4 guns) Battery not at Gettysburg

IMBODEN'S COMMAND
Brig.Gen. J.D. Imboden (2,245)
Guarding baggage, not involved at Gettysburg.
Field & Staff Officers: 4
18th Virginia Cavalry – Col. George H. Imboden (914)
62nd Virginia Infantry – Col. George H. Smith (1095)
Virginia Partisan Rangers – Capt. John H. McNeill (90)
Staunton Horse Arty. Virginia Btty – Capt. J.H. McClanahan (142)
Artillery – Brig.Gen. W.N. Pendleton (w/Ewell's Corps)

GETTYSBURG: DAY ONE

THE DECISION TO HOLD GETTYSBURG

On 30 June, just before noon, Union cavalry arrived at the southern edge of Gettysburg and Confederate General Pettigrew withdrew his troops from the western outskirts of town. He did not realize that the weary bluecoats were lead elements of Gen. John Buford's cavalry, the same men who had taken J.E.B. Stuart to task at Brandy Station and who were the eyes and ears of the Army of the Potomac. As his orders instructed him to avoid any serious conflict, Pettigrew withdrew west on the Chambersburg Pike and headed toward Cashtown to report to A.P. Hill, without engaging the enemy.

Buford's troopers had barely entered Gettysburg when nervous citizens accosted them with stories of Confederate soldiers west of town. Moreover, some citizens related how Confederates going east had passed through four days earlier. Buford was perhaps the best Union cavalry commander at Gettysburg, and as a professional soldier he evaluated reports of the enemy's proximity. While most of his men were on picket, broke out coffee and rations, or caught up on sleep, he began assessing his position. Too many Confederates were in the area – and the soldiers the people of Gettysburg were talking about were not cavalry patrols, so

Gettysburg, just five miles north of the Maryland border, was a small town and the county seat of an agricultural area of no military importance.

the men they had seen were more than just a reconnaissance. He did not know the Confederates' location, and although Gettysburg had no military importance, Buford recognized its strategic importance because of the roads which radiated from it.

As Buford saw it, Gettysburg was the key to central and eastern Pennsylvania. If Lee was to be stopped, it had to be here, before the town provided a base from which he could strike out in any direction. Like Waterloo, this placid farm town found itself of strategic importance not because of what it was, but where it was. Buford passed word to his unit commanders to set out pickets. He made plans for skirmish lines west of the city and then set up his command post at the Lutheran Seminary so he could use its tall spire as an observation post. For some reason the enemy had withdrawn, but since his unit had been spotted, he had to prepare and not allow the Confederates to occupy the town without a fight.

Reports indicated the presence of two Confederate units operating in the area, which might mean the Army of Northern Virginia was here. Preparing for that eventuality, Buford posted Col. William Gamble's brigade of 1,612 men west of town, on the south side of the railroad across the Chambersburg Road and on to Herr's Ridge (named after Herr's Tavern, at its crest) to watch the Cashtown Road. He ordered part of Col. Thomas Devin's second brigade to deploy to the north of the railroad cut and north up to Oak Hill, and then east to guard the approaches from Mummasberg, Carlisle, and York. Vedettes (mounted pickets) were positioned three to four miles ahead of the cavalry positions to report any advances of Southern troops either from the west (Hill) or from the north (Ewell).

Devin deployed his units north of town from right to left in the following order: 17th Pennsylvania, 9th New York, 6th New York, and two companies of the 3rd West Virginia. South of the Chambersburg Road Gamble deployed his men from left to right: 8th New York, 8th Illinois, four companies of the 12th Illinois, and six of the 3rd Indiana.

For every three men on the line of battle, a cavalryman stood 20 yards behind holding the reins of their horses and his own. This reduced Gamble's effectives by a quarter. Buford was no slash and dash old-school cavalryman, and he firmly believed that cavalry was mobile, mounted infantry that had the capability to move quickly to a location, dismount, and then fight dismounted as infantry.

Supporting Buford's two cavalry brigades was 1st Lt. John Calef's Battery A, 2nd US Horse Artillery, which totalled six three-inch rifles. The remainder of Buford's cavalry, the third brigade – under Gen. Wesley Merritt – was in reserve at Mechanicsburg. Behind fences and hedges Gamble's troopers watched for approaching Confederates, their fingers tight around their Sharps breechloading carbines. Gamble put Maj. William Beveridge's 8th Illinois on the ridge above on Marsh Creek, near the bridge in the reeds and weeds on its west bank, concealed by the shallow banks and foliage, a meagre and makeshift position almost three miles west of town. A brigade against a division or corps, even in ambush, presented terrible odds.

Despite troopers who were, in his words, "fagged out," Buford sent scouts west and north to find the precise location of the Southern Army. The soldiers they had spotted west of town were not Stuart's raiders, but Confederate infantry. The reports of Confederates outside Harrisburg

Union uniforms originally favoured the Hardee hat and frock coats, but by Gettysburg they had been replaced by kepis, slouch hats and shorter issue "sack" coats.

and York made sense, as did these reports of westbound troops, who could not be the ones reported earlier east of town. He suspected Lee's forces were split, or had been and were trying to reunite and situate themselves nearby. If that was true, the enemy was not massed but divided.

When Buford's scouts returned late that night, they reported massed Confederate troops nine miles away at Cashtown, and Buford knew the game of cat and mouse was over. If reports about Confederates at York and Harrisburg were accurate, and if the Confederate infantry he had seen were regulars, he knew his small force was between the hammer and anvil of the Confederate Army. Gettysburg seemed a logical target for a Confederate offensive, for if they controlled these crossroads, their movement options were immense. Knowing the location of Pettigrew's men, he dispatched riders not only to Gen. Meade, but also to the closest Union commander, Maj.Gen. John F. Reynolds, who commanded I Corps. Buford needed support to hold Gettysburg if the Southerners were to be stopped. Now that his troopers were positioned, all he could do was wait until reinforcements came. With luck, they would arrive before Lee's army.

That evening one of Buford's commanders remarked that he thought the Confederates were foragers and nothing more, and that with their men in defensive positions, they could easily beat off the Confederates if they came back. Buford, a realist, listened quietly and then disagreed, "No, you won't. They will attack you in the morning, and they will come booming – skirmishers three deep. You will have to fight like the devil to survive."

Buford's dispatches first reached Gen. Reynolds' I Corps. They were

HETH ATTACKS, 1 JULY, 1863

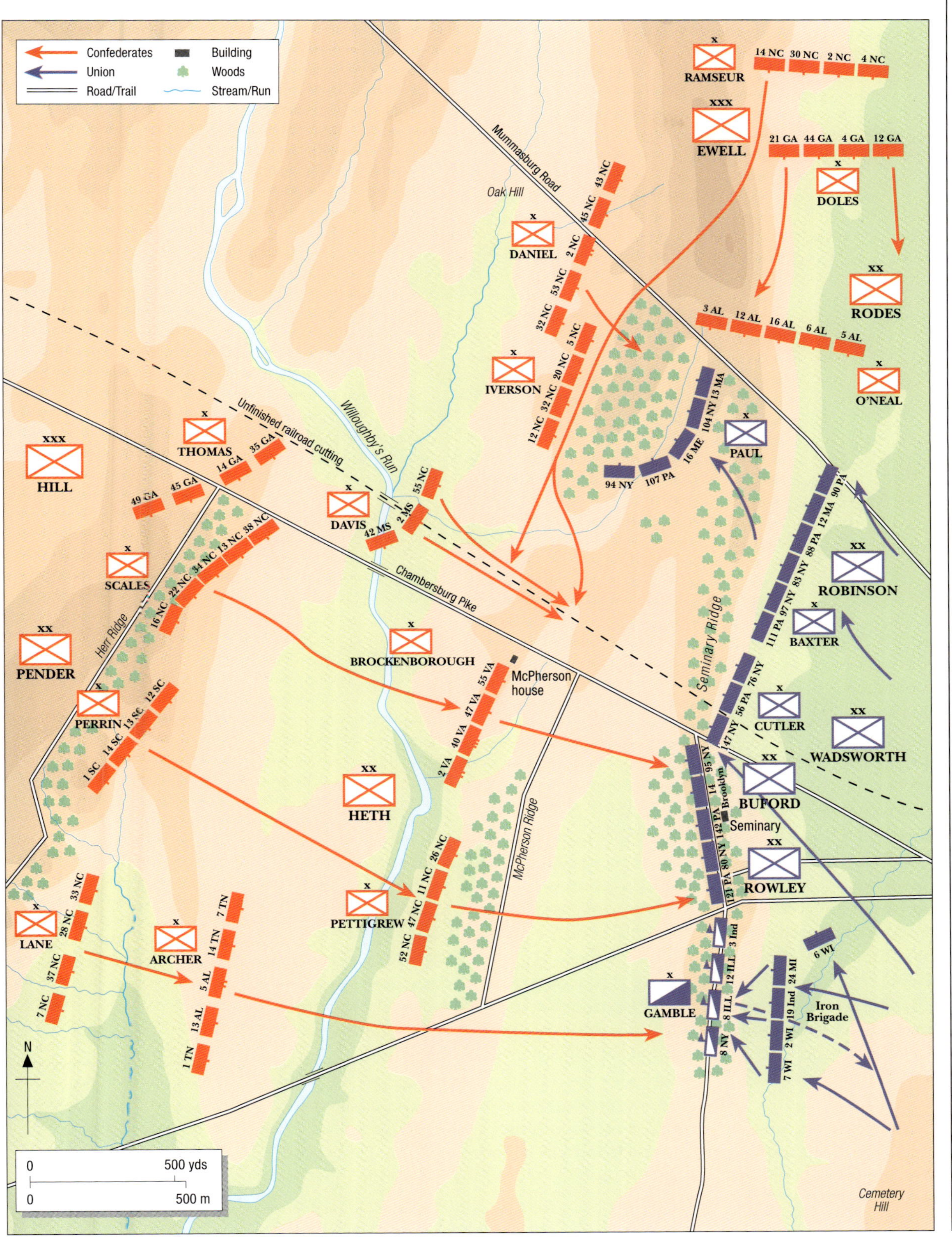

The overcoat with cape provided good protection and warmth but was bulky. It was often discarded in favour of a blanket roll and gun blanket in the field.

bivouacked 11 miles south of Gettysburg at Emmitsburg. Reynolds studied Buford's report and tried to decide what Lee might do. Lee might go to Gettysburg, or he might capture Harrisburg, or search out the Army of the Potomac, or even evade Meade and thrust down at Washington. To counteract a Southern offensive from Gettysburg, Reynolds put his men in position to defend against an attack from the north. A 20-year veteran, Reynolds not only commanded I Corps, but was also in charge of the movements of Gen. Daniel Sickles' III Corps and Gen. O.O. Howard's XI Corps. His command encompassed nearly 33,000 effectives, almost a third of the Army of the Potomac. Once his men were moving into position, Reynolds sent Buford's intelligence back to Gen. Meade who was encamped 12 miles south of Emmitsburg. Along with Buford's report, Reynolds sent his recommendation that Meade move the rest of the army up to Emmitsburg and that they form there to meet a likely Confederate attack from Gettysburg.

Meade read Buford's report and Reynolds' recommendation. He saw no clear indication of what Lee would do. Meade had three options: contest Gettysburg, form a defence at Emmitsburg, or order his troops to retire and form up at Pipe Creek, which afforded a better defensive position than

Emmitsburg. He did not like the ground they would have to fight on at Emmitsburg and dismissed that option. Simply put, he could either fall back or advance, and he agonized over the choice, even preparing two sets of orders, one for each option. In the early hours of morning, Meade decided that Lee counted on the Army of the Potomac being hesitant because of Hooker's past actions and his recent assumption of command. [Lee felt that Meade would make no mistakes and that he could afford to make none either.] Meade knew that if his actions were predictable, Lee had the advantage. Lincoln wanted the Army of the Potomac to be aggressive, and if that's what the president wanted, that's what he'd get. He decided to meet Lee head-on at Gettysburg, and sent those orders to his commanders. His plan called for Reynolds and Howard to advance immediately and for four other Union commanders to move there as quickly as possible to support them.

That evening Reynolds ordered Brig.Gen. James Wadsworth to take his 1st Division, I Corps (3,860 men), towards Gettysburg to reinforce Buford. This was composed of the 1st Brigade (The Iron Brigade) which was battle-proven and wore distinctive black slouch hats, and Cutler's 2nd Brigade of seasoned men. Major-general Abner Doubleday was to follow and bring up the rest of his corps (7,738 men). Orders were sent for XI Corps to follow and for III Corps to move into a support position upon arriving at Gettysburg. Although Wadsworth left early on 1 July, Doubleday did not get his men moving until 0800 hours that day.

Upon arriving at Gettysburg, Reynolds correctly assessed the situation and sent Meade word that he had to fight or leave this town to the Confederates.

OPENING CONFEDERATE MOVES

After withdrawing from Gettysburg, Pettigrew reported to his superior, Gen. Henry Heth, and III Corps commander, Gen. A.P. Hill, that Union cavalry had been seen entering the town. Heth listened attentively and A.P. Hill mulled over Pettigrew's words. Confederate intelligence placed the Army of the Potomac at Middleburg; therefore, they reasoned that if there were Yankees in Gettysburg, they were state militia or a scouting detachment, but probably not the Army of the Potomac. Since Pettigrew had not captured any Union troops, he could not offer any other suggestion. Satisfied with this analysis, Heth asked Hill if he had any objection to Heth's occupation of the town because his men needed shoes badly and according to rumours there was a warehouse full of them in Gettysburg. Hill shook his head, saying, "None in the world."

The morning of 1 July, 1863, was warm, and sunrise was at 0515 hours. By then, columns of Heth's division were already on the Chambersburg Road heading east. Heth ordered the brigades of Archer, Pettigrew, Brockenborough, and Davis to advance towards Gettysburg. Major William Pegram's and Maj. G.D. McIntosh's artillery accompanied Heth. Archer's brigade of nearly 1,200 men was in the lead, followed by Davis' 2,241 men, Pettigrew's 2,581 men, and Brockenborough's 971 men – in that order.

At Marsh Creek, Archer sent out Col. Fry's 13th Alabama Regiment

Abner Doubleday was relieved of his corps command because Howard mistakenly reported that his men were fleeing the battlefield and seemed leaderless.

BUFORD'S CAVALRY HOLD HETH'S ADVANCE, 1 July

Just after dawn, pickets of the 8th Illinois cavalry saw dim forms approaching their position on the Chambersburg Road in the early morning mist. 1st Lt. Marcellus Jones, realizing they were Confederates, fired on Heth's lead elements and then withdrew. This was the first of many such Union delaying tactics on the first day of Gettysburg.

of 308 men and Maj. Van de Graff's 135 men of the 5th Alabama Battalion as skirmishers south of the pike. A gentle rain increased the discomfort of the 70° dawn, and steam rose from the roads, creating a ground fog which limited visibility. Soldiers' shirts were sodden and the sun scorched both the advancing Confederates and watchful Union cavalry pickets. Beveridge's troopers waited until the advancing infantry had been firmly identified as Confederates, and then opened fire on 1st Lt. Maracellus Jones' command. Jones' first shot was at a mounted Confederate officer. The Alabamians returned fire, and the battle of Gettysburg began. It was barely 0530 hours.

For the next two hours the Confederates advanced steadily, pausing to load their muzzle-loading Enfields while Union cavalrymen popped away with their Sharps breechloaders and .44 caliber Colt revolvers. The gray tide crept forward, and despite superior firepower, the Union troopers slowly began withdrawing before the overwhelming Southern numbers, pausing to fire, reload, and fire again before moving a few more paces backward.

North of the turnpike, Heth deployed Brig.Gen. Joseph R. Davis' brigade, and south he deployed Archer's brigade in the lead. Steadily they advanced, firing, and wary lest other Union troops were concealed in ambush. They followed the Union troopers who were slowly giving ground – holding up the Confederate advance with small arms fire and then falling back. So effective was the Union resistance that it took the

Confederates over two hours to advance from Marsh Creek to Willoughby Run, a distance of less than a mile.

By 0800 Heth had just reached the crest of Herr's Ridge. His two lead brigades moved confidently down the east slope towards McPherson's Ridge and were almost at Willoughby Run when Gamble's troopers who had been concealed in weeds and brush opened fire. Calef's battery added the screech of 6-inch rifles to the din. Even though the Confederates faltered at the first blast, they doggedly pushed forward. Sheer weight of numbers allowed them to cross the ford, but their advance faltered on the east bank under the constant outpouring of carbine fire. At Oak Hill, Devin's men came under fire from advance elements of Rodes' brigade moving down from the north. Colonel William Sackett's 9th New York cavalry (561 men), a forward element of Devin's skirmishers, was among the first units engaged.

Because of the inexperience of the Confederates, the odd angle of the creek in relation to the road, and the uneven resistance of the Union cavalry, a peculiar situation developed. As the Confederates pushed east, the division between Davis' and Archer's brigades widened. Instead of attacking the Union line as a line, the action devolved into two piecemeal attacks that greatly diminished the effectiveness of the Confederate assault despite their vast numerical superiority and allowed the Union cavalrymen to fight two separate withdrawing actions.

Major William Pegram moved three guns of his battery into place on Belmont Schoolhouse Ridge when he heard the Union artillery open fire. Quickly locating the Union position on McPherson Ridge, he ordered his men to fire on Calef's battery at long range. Calef's gunners returned fire, and for nearly an hour the sounds of carbine, musket and field-piece shattered the morning. Slowly the Southerners inched their way east to higher ground.

Buford was watching from the steeple of the seminary. By 0900 he realized that the relentless Confederates would push across Willoughby Run. He looked around and noted a few men in blue galloping toward the sound of the guns and his position – Maj.Gen. John Reynolds had arrived. "The devil's to pay," Buford yelled down to him, explaining what was happening across on McPherson's Ridge. Reynolds asked Buford if he could hold a while longer as reinforcements were coming. "I reckon I can," Buford replied grimly.

Reynolds sent a dispatch to Meade at Taneytown. "The enemy is advancing in strong force," he noted, referring to McPherson's Ridge. "I will fight him inch by inch, and if driven into the town I will barricade the streets and hold him back as long as possible." This was what Meade wanted to hear, for it mirrored his own determination not to flee from the Army of Northern Virginia but to stand and fight Lee toe to toe if need be. Then Reynolds wheeled his horse and galloped out of town and south, searching for Wadsworth.

A.P. Hill was in poor health throughout the war, perhaps suffering from a psychosomatic illness which often debilitated him before an engagement.

REYNOLDS' DEATH

About a mile south of town, Reynolds encountered Wadsworth's brigades and the 2nd Maine battery commanded by Maj. J.A. Hall. Immediately he ordered Cutler's 2nd Brigade and Meredith's 1st

Just beyond the pond, part-way to the trees, was where Reynolds turned in his saddle to urge the men of the 2nd Wisconsin forward when a bullet struck him behind the ear, killing him instantly.

Brigade (The Iron Brigade) to move cross-country to the ridges west of town, where they could hear firing. An orderly called to Wadsworth, "The Rebs are thicker'n blackberries ahead." Wadsworth's men dropped their knapsacks, and took off double-time, loading muskets as they jogged toward McPherson's Ridge, arriving at its crest at about 1000 hours. The artillery headed cross country in a jingle of harness.

Hall's artillery reached McPherson Ridge first. They unlimbered south of the railroad cut and were determined to aid Calef in counter-battery fire against Pegram. The artillerymen were loading their 3-inch rifles when the 511 men of the 42nd Mississippi rose from the railroad cut and fired into them. Without hesitation, Hall wheeled his guns to face north and raked the Confederates with canister at a range of 50 yards, sending the survivors dashing for the cover offered by the cut's embankment.

Reynolds arrived on the scene and ordered two of Cutler's rear guard, the 84th New York (14th Brooklyn, dressed as French-style chasseurs in blue jackets and red trousers) and the 95th New York, to the western crest of the ridge to relieve Buford's men, who were in an area roughly triangulated between McPherson's house, his barn, and McPherson's Woods to the south of the outbuildings. He held the 6th Wisconsin as a reserve. In the confusion, the 147th New York was over-looked and no orders were issued, so its commander, Lt.Col. Francis C. Miller, massed it behind McPherson's barn.

A little after 1000 hours Cutler's 2nd Brigade reached the eastern

BATTLE OF GETTYSBURG

1 July 1863, 0800 - 1500, viewed from the south-east showing the Confederate assaults from the north and north-west and the Union's fighting retreat

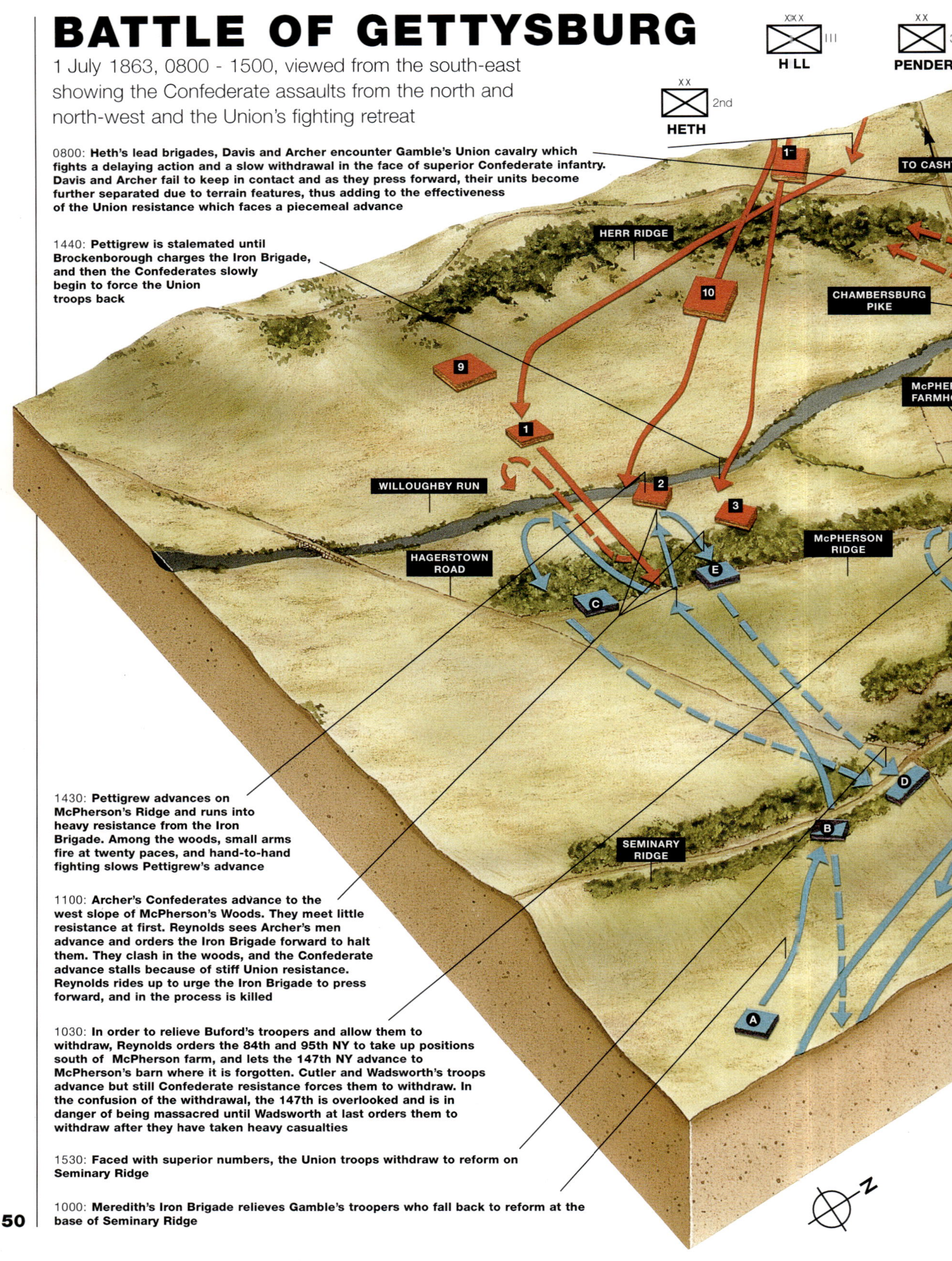

0800: **Heth's lead brigades, Davis and Archer encounter Gamble's Union cavalry which fights a delaying action and a slow withdrawal in the face of superior Confederate infantry. Davis and Archer fail to keep in contact and as they press forward, their units become further separated due to terrain features, thus adding to the effectiveness of the Union resistance which faces a piecemeal advance**

1440: **Pettigrew is stalemated until Brockenborough charges the Iron Brigade, and then the Confederates slowly begin to force the Union troops back**

1430: **Pettigrew advances on McPherson's Ridge and runs into heavy resistance from the Iron Brigade. Among the woods, small arms fire at twenty paces, and hand-to-hand fighting slows Pettigrew's advance**

1100: **Archer's Confederates advance to the west slope of McPherson's Woods. They meet little resistance at first. Reynolds sees Archer's men advance and orders the Iron Brigade forward to halt them. They clash in the woods, and the Confederate advance stalls because of stiff Union resistance. Reynolds rides up to urge the Iron Brigade to press forward, and in the process is killed**

1030: **In order to relieve Buford's troopers and allow them to withdraw, Reynolds orders the 84th and 95th NY to take up positions south of McPherson farm, and lets the 147th NY advance to McPherson's barn where it is forgotten. Cutler and Wadsworth's troops advance but still Confederate resistance forces them to withdraw. In the confusion of the withdrawal, the 147th is overlooked and is in danger of being massacred until Wadsworth at last orders them to withdraw after they have taken heavy casualties**

1530: **Faced with superior numbers, the Union troops withdraw to reform on Seminary Ridge**

1000: **Meredith's Iron Brigade relieves Gamble's troopers who fall back to reform at the base of Seminary Ridge**

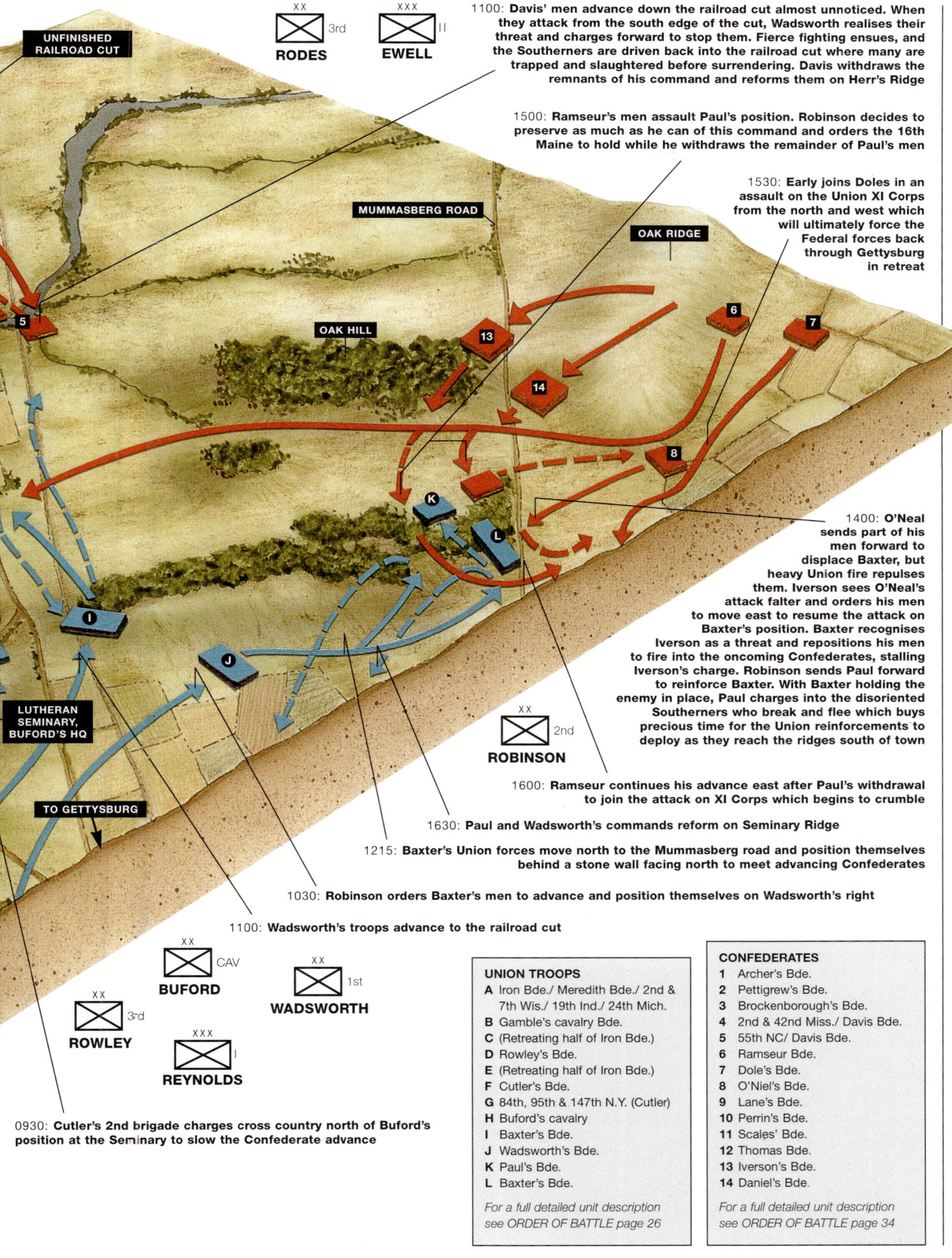

UNION TROOPS

- **A** Iron Bde./ Meredith Bde./ 2nd & 7th Wis./ 19th Ind./ 24th Mich.
- **B** Gamble's cavalry Bde.
- **C** (Retreating half of Iron Bde.)
- **D** Rowley's Bde.
- **E** (Retreating half of Iron Bde.)
- **F** Cutler's Bde.
- **G** 84th, 95th & 147th N.Y. (Cutler)
- **H** Buford's cavalry
- **I** Baxter's Bde.
- **J** Wadsworth's Bde.
- **K** Paul's Bde.
- **L** Baxter's Bde.

For a full detailed unit description see ORDER OF BATTLE page 26

CONFEDERATES

- **1** Archer's Bde.
- **2** Pettigrew's Bde.
- **3** Brockenborough's Bde.
- **4** 2nd & 42nd Miss./ Davis Bde.
- **5** 55th NC/ Davis Bde.
- **6** Ramseur Bde.
- **7** Dole's Bde.
- **8** O'Niel's Bde.
- **9** Lane's Bde.
- **10** Perrin's Bde.
- **11** Scales' Bde.
- **12** Thomas Bde.
- **13** Iverson's Bde.
- **14** Daniel's Bde.

For a full detailed unit description see ORDER OF BATTLE page 34

slope of McPherson's Ridge. Wadsworth ordered the 76th New York and the 56th Pennsylvania north of the pike to defend Hall's guns. They encountered the 55th North Carolina and engaged in a firefight. Davis positioned the 2nd Mississippi on the 55th North Carolina's right and together they charged, partially enfilading the Union line. In the mêlée, the 76th New York lost 234 of its 375 men. As they had no orders, Miller saw where the 147th New York was needed and moved them across the road to take a position on the 56th Pennsylvania's left just as the 42nd Mississippi charged. The roar of musket-fire was intense. Wadsworth ordered his units to retire. Before Lt.Col. Miller of the 147th New York could pass the order to withdraw, he was shot through the throat; in the din of battle, the 147th did not see the 56th Pennsylvania and 76th New York withdraw, and so both they and Hall's battery stood their ground.

At distances of between six and eight yards the enemies traded fire and the Confederates pressed their advantage. Hall fired his guns, limbered and pulled out section by section, braving a crossfire Hall later described as "hellish." Wadsworth had seen the 147th's plight and dispatched an aide to again order them to withdraw. This time the order was understood and the survivors of the 147th flooded eastward in disarray, leaving three quarters of their strength dead or disabled.

Archer's troops surged up the slope toward McPherson's Woods. Reynolds saw their advance. Looking desperately around, he located the Iron Brigade, which had just moved into the depression between Seminary Ridge and McPherson's Ridge. He waved them up the slope towards the woods, shouting, "Forward men, forward, for God's sake, and drive those fellows out of those woods." Archer's 1,197 men charged through the woods, intent on flanking the Union line. Meredith's Iron Brigade loaded as they dashed up the slope and into the eastern edge of the woods. Reynolds followed the 302 men of the 2nd Wisconsin towards the woods. Union and Confederate lines unleashed tremendous volleys at each other. Reynolds turned in his saddle, intent on finding more troops to send forward when the volleys were fired. A bullet struck him behind the right ear, sending him reeling in his saddle, and he died before he touched the ground. Maj.Gen. Abner Doubleday now commanded I Corps.

The Midwestern troops of the Iron Brigade surged past the fallen corps commander and into the woods. Viewing themselves as an elite fighting unit, members of the Iron Brigade wore distinctive black slouch hats. An orderly yelled, "Hold the grove at all costs." A member of the Iron Brigade replied, "If we cannot... where will you find men who can?"

Archer's men poured across Willoughby Run and into the trees. The 2nd Wisconsin's fire slowed their advance but a moment. The Confederates fired at 40 yards and Solomon Meredith fell wounded. The Iron Brigade – undaunted – paused, returned fire, and then continued their charge. As Confederates reloaded and fired at the still advancing Federals, one muttered in disbelief that they hadn't broken and run and were coming back for more. "There are those damned black-hatted fellows again." One of his sharper-eyed companions exclaimed, "T'ain't no militia. It's the Army of the Potomac!"

The 800 or more men of the 19th Indiana and 24th Michigan fired into the Confederate flank, and although the Southerners returned their fire, the battle-hardened Iron Brigade withstood the volley. Then

This Michigan regiment in field uniforms (possibly the 24th Michigan, part of the Iron Brigade) wears black slouch hats – like those that members of the Iron Brigade wore in preference to kepis.

they fired and continued their push so that Archer's advance first faltered and then changed into a withdrawal to the western slope of the ford. In the battle, the 24th Michigan's flag fell 14 times as standard bearers were killed or disabled. The Iron Brigade followed closely and engaged the rearmost Confederates in mêlée. Contact was so close that Pte. Patrick Mahoney of the 2nd Wisconsin captured Gen. Archer.

On his way to the rear, Archer passed Doubleday, who was glad to see an acquaintance alive and unharmed and extended his hand, saying, "I'm glad to see you." Archer, understandably angry, muttered, "Well, I'm not glad to see you by a damn sight!"

Howard takes charge

Meanwhile, Wadsworth watched the disintegration of the Union line near the railroad cut as the 147th pulled out after Hall's artillery was safely away. From the roof of Fahnestock's Mercantile, Gen. O.O. Howard also witnessed the retreat of Cutler's units, but mistakenly believed the entire I Corps to be routing! He reported this mistaken belief to Meade, which resulted in Doubleday temporarily being relieved of command. The Confederates in the railroad cut hesitated and then began moving south toward the Chambersburg Pike. Wadsworth sent an aide to the commander of the 6th Wisconsin, Lt.Col. Rufus Dawes, ordering him to take the 344 men of the 6th to plug the gap to the right, adding, "Go like hell!"

As the 6th Wisconsin double-timed north across the field, they saw the gray tide flow over the south bank of the railroad cut toward them. Reaching the south edge of the pike, they rested their muskets on the rail fence bordering it and aimed at the Confederates advancing from across the road. They fired, and their volley staggered the Confederate line, which recoiled and then retreated to the safety of the cut swiftly pursued by Dawes' men as they crossed the rail fences.

The 95th New York and 84th New York hit the Confederates from the left. The Union regiments hit in echelon – three staggering collisions of men. Seeing what the Union was doing, Davis ordered his men to withdraw from the cut, but many did not receive his orders and remained. The remnants of his brigade re-formed on Herr's Ridge. For those who stayed, the hand-to-hand fighting and point-blank volleys into the railroad cut withered the remaining Confederate resistance. Finally Dawes made himself heard and yelled for the Confederates to surrender. Nearly 250 Southerners dropped their weapons. It was only 1100 hours.

Lee was near South Mountain when he heard the distant artillery fire. He neither planned nor wanted a full scale engagement unless he could bring the full might of the Army of Northern Virginia to bear, and Longstreet was behind him, Hill before him, and Ewell was backtracking from the east. No one knew where Stuart was. At Cashtown Lee located a sick A.P. Hill, and only then learned of Hill and Heth's decision to engage in a major battle against Lee's wishes. He had reason to be concerned, for his army was spread over 60 or more linear miles and was escalating an engagement with an enemy whose strength was unknown, while the Army of the Potomac was about somewhere, waiting to pounce. He voiced his displeasure at Stuart's absence and mounted his gray horse, Traveller, to march to the sound of the guns.

After this maelstrom of combat, which culminated in the surrender at the railroad cut, a lull fell over the battleground for the next two hours. Both sides regrouped and deployed fresh units to strengthen their lines. Doubleday moved Robinson's 2nd Division and two artillery batteries into reserve on Seminary Ridge and positioned his own 3rd Division (now commanded by Brig.Gen. Thomas Rowley) and two batteries on McPherson Ridge. Colonel Roy Stone's 2nd Brigade (the Bucktail Brigade) formed on the western crest, to the right of the Iron Brigade, extending the Union line fully from the woods to the Chambersburg Pike. The 1st Brigade, now commanded by Col. Chapman Biddle, formed on the eastern crest of the ridge to the left rear of the Iron Brigade. When Buford repositioned Gamble's cavalry, he moved it too far south and east, exposing Biddle's left flank.

Howard informed Doubleday that he was assuming command of the Union Army, and he told Doubleday to have I Corps hold the left. Howard intended to have Doubleday extend his right flank by moving two of his divisions to Oak Hill once the line was secure. Howard then ordered XI Corps to advance and take up position in the farmlands and low ridges north of Gettysburg. Finally, he established his headquarters on Cemetery Hill, because the hill and its neighboring ridge (Cemetery Ridge) were the high ground which effectively controlled the town. By 1230 hours all of XI Corps (now commanded by Schurz) and its artillery brigade were at the southern edge of Gettysburg, on the Taneytown and Emmitsburg roads, preparing to move north through town.

Howard received a report that Confederates were in strength on Oak Hill, and he changed his plans for Doubleday, instead ordering Steinwehr's 3rd Division and two batteries to be a ready reserve on Cemetery Hill, while Barlow's 1st Division and Schimmelpfennig's 2nd Division and two batteries were to take positions north of town to oppose the Confederate advance. Schurz was to oversee movements of XI Corps, while Howard commanded the entire field. It took the 1st and 2nd

THE DEATH OF GEN. REYNOLDS, 1 JULY

After Buford advised him of the Confederate skirmishers to the south and west, Reynolds located Union troops entering Gettysburg from the south and double-timed them across fields to block the Confederate advance. Realizing this was a full-scale assault and not a scouting party, Reynolds urged Union troops at hand forward into the woods. As he turned in his saddle to locate more reinforcements a bullet struck him behind the ear, killing him instantly.

The railroad cut (at the time of the battle) was unfinished to the west of town. It first provided shelter from which the Confederates attacked McPherson's Ridge, but later became a death trap, when Union troops fired down into it at the Southerners.

divisions more than an hour to move through town and onto the farmlands north of town.

Rodes' Confederates moved toward Oak Hill about noon. They were weary, having had Ewell change their marching orders while they were en route, and they took nearly two hours to form a line of battle. Lieutenant-colonel Thomas Carter arrived at the top of Oak Hill before the bulk of Rodes' men and used the flat top of the hill as an artillery park, bringing the assorted 16 guns of the 3rd Division Artillery to bear on the Union troops now massing north of Gettysburg and on McPherson Ridge.

When Schurz gave Barlow orders to advance, he did not intend for Barlow to move so far ahead, occupying the west, north and east sides of a low knoll near Rock Creek. Schimmelpfennig's brigades of 1,638 men extended to the southwest, almost to the crest of Oak Hill, where part of Doubleday's I Corps was moving into position. Doubleday ordered Baxter to move his men from the Lutheran Seminary to the northern end of Oak Ridge, along the Mummasberg Road, which followed the contour of Oak Hill. They formed behind a stone wall that faced north.

At about 1400 hours Rodes ordered the attack. Colonel O'Neal's brigade of Alabamians led the assault. O'Neal used only three of his five brigades, charging en masse at a narrow front held by Baxter's 2nd Brigade. As the Confederates charged, Baxter's men fired repeated volleys from behind the wall, driving the Confederates back. Almost as soon as it had begun, O'Neal's assault ended in defeat.

Seeing the Alabamians' plight, Brig.Gen. Alfred Iverson ordered his brigade, composed of the 5th, 12th, 20th and 23rd North Carolina, to take the wall. Iverson did not send skirmishers ahead. Baxter saw the coming assault and relocated his men behind a stone wall at the crest of Oak Ridge, facing west. Iverson's North Carolinians moved forward in parade-ground formation. Some of Cutler's men opened fire, driving the Confederates away from the base of the ridge and close to the stone wall where Baxter was concealed. At a range of 50 yards seemingly the entire crest erupted in a muzzle flash of brimstone before the startled Confederates when Baxter's men opened fire.

LEFT **After Reynolds' death, responsibility for the Union troops at Gettysburg fell on Howard, who rallied troops and tried to keep the Union line from falling into chaos. He organized the withdrawal to, and defense of, Culp's Hill.**

LINE OFFICERS GALLERY

Some of the principal participants who served at Gettysburg

UNION ARMY

John Buford realized the vast military importance of Gettysburg: from it radiated a dozen roads which gave whoever controlled it access to all major cities.

Brigadier-general Solomon Meredith commanded the 1st Brigade (the Iron Brigade) of I Corps. Reynolds encountered Meredith and Cutler and sent their men double-timing across the country fields to block the Confederates pouring down the Chambersburg Pike and onto McPherson Ridge.

Brigadier-general Lysander Cutler split his force to stop the Southern advance. Two units relieved Buford's weary cavalrymen while two others moved toward the railroad cut to support Hall's guns; a fifth was overlooked and left without orders in the escalating battle and was badly mauled.

Major-general Carl Schultz arrived at Gettysburg in time to assume command of XI Corps and at Howard's orders occupied northern ridges between Oak Hill and Barlow's Knoll about noon on July 1st.

Joshua Chamberlain was a teacher who left Bowdoin College to go to war. His bold action held Little Round Top and preserved the Union defence. After the war, he was elected governor of Maine and became president of the college where he had taught.

John Burns, Gettysburg's 70-year-old town constable, fought side by side with the 150th Pennsylvania and the 7th Wisconsin over the three days. He was wounded three times. President Lincoln came to see him afterwards, and Congress awarded him an $8 a month pension.

Brigadier Alexander Schimmelpfennig's men retreated into Gettysburg. Many were trapped in unfamiliar streets and surrendered. To escape capture, Schimmelpfennig hid in a woodpile until July 4th.

Colonel Regis de Trobriand was a poet, an artist, and a fine military commander whose men withstood the Confederate onslaught north of the Wheat Field until reinforced.

CONFEDERATE ARMY

Jubal Early was Lee's irascible "bad old man" who cursed, "chawed terbaccy," and together with Ewell sent Union Gen. Milroy fleeing Winchester for the safety of Harper's Ferry at the beginning of the Gettysburg campaign.

Henry Heth was an old enough and a close enough friend to Robert E. Lee to be one of only a very few men Lee called by his first name.

Brigadier Junius Daniel's plan was to follow the Chambersburg Pike's north side and then cut south to surprise the Union troops. However, he was unaware of the railroad cut, which threw his plans out of kilter.

John Bell Hood did not like the orders Longstreet gave him to roll up the Union flank by moving down the Emmitsburg Road, so he issued his own orders to his men, which led them into the Wheat Field and Devil's Den.

Longstreet felt McLaws was his most reliable commander. Together with Hood, McLaws' units spearheaded the attacks on the southern end of the Union line on July 2nd, 1863.

Evander Law was Hood's 1st Brigade commander. When Hood's arm was shattered at the beginning of the battle for the Wheat Field, Law took over command of Hood's division.

Brigadier Stephen D. Ramseur's North Carolinians so battered the Union troops at Oak Hill that Schimmelpfennig's line crumbled and was routed.

General Ambrose Wright's men captured two Union cannon and defeated two II Corps regiments, driving them back to Cemetery Ridge.

ABOVE **Roy Stone commanded the 2nd Division of Doubleday's III Corps, known as the Bucktails. They were so-called because members were crack shots and wore the tails of buck deer attached to their hats.**

Brigadier Thomas Rowley (shown here in his uniform as a colonel of the 102nd Regiment) ordered his troops to take two artillery batteries and position themselves on McPherson Ridge.

OPPOSITE **General Rodes was diverted from the planned Cashtown rendezvous to Gettysburg but with the caveat not to bring on a general engagement. An aggressive commander, he came in from the northeast and headed to Oak Hill, where XI Corps engaged Doles' of his command.**

When the powder smoke cleared, hundreds of dead and dying Confederates lay in parade formation. Those in the rear and a few forward survivors took shelter in a gully 100 yards west of the stone fence, but the 20th North Carolina was pinned. Baxter charged part of his brigade down the slope firing, and captured nearly 400 North Carolinians. So devastating was Baxter's attack that only one officer of the 23rd North Carolina remained unbloodied. Remnants of Iverson's brigade fled north. O'Neal's Alabamians rallied, charged, and occupied the north section of the wall because Baxter's men were running out of ammunition. Robinson sent Brig.Gen. Gabriel Paul's brigade to Baxter's defence.

Paul's regiments formed a right angle where the Mummasberg Road met Oak Ridge. Carter's artillery and the Confederate infantry poured fire into the reinforcing Yankees. Paul positioned his brigade from right to left with the 13th Massachusetts on the lower east slope of Oak Ridge facing north and the 104th New York on the upper slope extending the line. Facing west were the 16th Maine, the 107th Pennsylvania, and the 94th New York. While positioning his men behind the stone walls, Paul was hit by a bullet which destroyed both his eyes. Shortly thereafter, the Confederates overran the angle, driving the Union back.

After Paul lost his eyes, Col. Leonard assumed command but he soon fell wounded and Col. Root of the 94th New York took over. Root too was wounded, so Col. Coulter of the 11th Pennsylvania took command until he too was hit. Finally Col. Lyle became commander of the 1st Brigade. The fire from the Southerners was terrible, especially from the angle. Col. Prey of the 104th rallied his men, telling them they all would die if they failed to re-take the angle. His men hesitated, until he moved to the front rank yelling, "I'll lead you, boys." The 104th recaptured the angle, but so far that day they had already lost seven standard bearers to enemy fire. Thereafter Paul's brigade made several costly assaults to drive Iverson's newly reinforced men from the field, but in the end they only delayed the inevitable Confederate advance.

Heth regrouped his command while Pegram, March, and Carter's artillery pummeled the Union troops on McPherson Ridge. Between 1400 and 1430 the Confederate artillery blasted away at the Union position, and when the barrage lifted, Heth sent Brockenborough and Pettigrew forward to the farm outbuildings and the woods respectively.

THE UNION WITHDRAWS

About this time Robert E. Lee arrived at Marsh Creek. Heth told him, "Rodes is heavily engaged." Pausing long enough for Lee to assimilate the news, he asked, "Had I better not attack?" Lee replied, "I am not prepared to bring on a general engagement today." By way of explanation Lee said, "Longstreet is not up." Heth nodded and returned to Herr Ridge. When Doubleday engaged Rodes, Heth again requested permission to attack, and this time Lee gave him permission to send Pettigrew and Brockenborough forward.

Heth was wearing his new hat (which was too large and had been stuffed with papers by his orderly so it would fit better) and leading his men when a shot knocked him from the saddle and sent his hat flying.

Rushing to his aid, his officers saw that he had a nasty bruise and was unconscious, but that the paper had deflected the bullet so he only had a cracked skull instead of a fatal wound. With Heth unconscious, Pettigrew assumed command.

Pettigrew's North Carolinians charged McPherson Woods, where the Iron Brigade stood. The Iron Brigade reported that Pettigrew's men charged "yelling like demons." Despite desperate volleys and fierce hand-to-hand fighting, the 24th Michigan slowly withdrew as the Confederates, led by the 24th North Carolina, pressed into the woods. The 24th North Carolina slammed into the 151st Pennsylvania and exchanged murderous volleys at 20 yards. Brockenborough's Virginians ran into the Bucktails, who were already locked in combat with Brig.Gen. Junius Daniel's brigade. Brockenborough's attack turned the day in favour of the South, and Stone's Bucktails withdrew to re-form on Seminary Ridge. To the right, Pettigrew's attack turned Biddle's flank. This made the Iron Brigade's left flank vulnerable, and so it withdrew from the woods. Doubleday took the remnants of six brigades and formed a line on Seminary Ridge.

Colonel E.A. O'Neal ordered his men to charge headfirst against massed Union volleys from Baxter's defensive position, which quickly turned the charge into a retreat.

ABOVE **Brigadier-general Alfred Iverson saw O'Neal's men retreat under withering fire. Iverson's men moved to attack Cutler's troops and found themselves under small arms crossfire.**

LEFT **Brigadier-general Adolph von Steinwehr, late of the German Army, assumed his position on Cemetery Hill and immediately had his men digging rifle pits and gun emplacements among the tombstones and monuments.**

As Doubleday was pushing units into position, Heth's second division, under Pender, came across McPherson Ridge in perfect parade-ground formation, rank upon rank of fresh troops. Left to right were Thomas (north of Chambersburg Pike), Scales, Perrin, and Lane's brigades (all south of the pike). Union artillery blasted the charging Confederates, decimating Scales' command staff. A lone field officer rallied the men and they slowly re-formed. Perrin's men reached the Union lines and broke through Biddle's unit, enfilading the entire Union line. Doubleday realized his position was untenable and ordered a withdrawal – cannons first, to save the guns if he could, and then infantry. I Corps withdrew into town from the west.

To the north of town the Union XI Corps was hammered. While Rodes' troops held them in place, they were hit on their right flank by Early, whose troops had arrived at 1500 hours from the Harrisburg road, clobbering Barlow's exposed position and beginning to fold the Union line. Doles and Ramseur faced off against Schimmelpfennig, while three brigades, under Gordon, Hays and Avery, began to take the Union line in reverse. Suddenly Doles' Georgians, who had been facing Schimmelpfennig's men, moved to their left and also engaged Barlow. Schimmelpfennig sent a brigade to hit Doles' exposed flank, and Gordon's Georgians charged across the Wheat Field ulating a rebel yell. Battered on three sides, Barlow's division withdrew south from the knoll to the almshouse.

Colonel Abner Perrin's Carolinians relieved Heth's men and pressed the attack, receiving a cheer from tired Southerners. Drawing his sword, Perrin urged his men forward, and even though he was mounted and drawing both rifle and artillery fire, he remained uninjured on that day.

Meanwhile Paul's brigade on Oak Ridge was under fierce attack by Ramseur. Robinson ordered them back, leaving only the 16th Maine at the angle with orders to hold it "at any cost." Besieged by four regiments, the 16th Maine stood fast, losing 232 (77%) of its 298 men. Surrounded, the survivors shredded their flag to keep it out of Confederate hands and escaped.

The loss of the angle let Ramseur attack the 75th Pennsylvania, which held Schimmelpfennig's left flank. In a dozen minutes, more than half the unit fell, and with it the Union line. Barlow and Schimmelpfennig's men began streaming back to the northern edge of Gettysburg pursued by Hays and Avery's 2,539 men. Howard rushed Col. Charles R. Coster's brigade of 1,217 New Yorkers to strengthen Barlow's right, but it was too late because Barlow had broken. Coster's men ran into Hays' and Avery's brigades.

Things were no better in town. The scene was reminiscent of First Manassas, where panic ruled the fleeing Union troops. Trapped in town where streets were unfamiliar and sometimes led to dead ends, many Union soldiers became disoriented and surrendered as Hays', Ramseur's and Perrin's men flooded in behind them. By 1630 it was over: Gettysburg had fallen and Perrin established his command center in the town square. Surviving Union troops made their way to Cemetery Hill, where Howard and Gen. Winfield Scott Hancock (who had been sent by Meade to assume command of the army) rallied them using Col. Orland Smith's brigade as a rallying point. By 1700 the dazed (but not demoralized) Union troops were re-formed on Cemetery Hill, overlooking Gettysburg.

Brigadier George Doles engaged Schimmelpfennig and then shifted to attack Barlow, a move ultimately putting Barlow under attack from three sides.

The Union defense was assuming its famous fishhook shape. By 1715 hours Wadsworth held Culp's Hill to the southeast, Doubleday held Cemetery Hill and Schurz's XI Corps held the east of Cemetery Hill.

Buford's cavalry lined the heights above the Emmitsburg Road to protect the Union flank. Hancock sent word to Meade that he could hold out until nightfall.

As Hancock's courier was riding south to find Meade, Maj.Gen. Henry Slocum's XII Corps came up the Baltimore Pike followed by lead elements of Sickles' III Corps moving up the Emmitsburg Road. Before nightfall Hancock's II Corps was bivouacked less than two miles from Cemetery Hill, near Little Round Top. Around 1830 hours Slocum assumed command of the army at Gettysburg. As night fell, the Union Army was in a good defensive position, perhaps the best it had been in all day, and the Confederate armies had stopped attacking. They did not know what tomorrow would bring, but for tonight the fighting was over.

Lee set up his command post at Seminary Ridge. He was studying the Federal position on Cemetery Hill when Longstreet arrived. After a brief discussion, Longstreet suggested a flanking action around the heights, to threaten Washington and throw the Yankees off balance. Lee disagreed, saying, "If the enemy is there (on the heights) tomorrow, I will

ABOVE **Brigadier-general William Dorsey Pender linked up with Heth and together with Early and Rodes of Ewell's Corps began to squeeze the Union XI Corps from the north and west.**

Hancock (seated) and his division commanders (left to right) Barlow, Birney and Gibbon. Each man in this picture was severely wounded during the fighting at Gettysburg.

attack him." Longstreet, who well understood defensive positioning, was dismayed. "If the enemy is there," he noted, "it is because he is anxious that we should attack him – a good reason in my judgement for not doing so."

Ewell was entering Gettysburg and conversing with Gen. Gordon when there was a slapping sound and he reeled in the saddle. Gen. Gordon saw no blood and inquired, "Are you hurt, sir?" "No," Ewell answered, gesturing to his artificial leg. "It don't hurt a bit to be shot in a wooden leg."

Lee sent Col. Walter Taylor, a staff officer, to Ewell, urging him to "press 'those people'... to secure possession of the heights," stating that he wished Ewell to do this. Ewell listened and did not voice any disagreement, so the officer returned to Lee with the assumption that Ewell would carry out Lee's orders. However, Ewell did not advance.

Perhaps three-quarters of an hour had passed since the capture of the town, and Ewell's men were worn out. He did not have time to reorganize them for a meticulous assault before reinforcements arrived. When Lee saw that Ewell did not move forward, he rode over to Ewell's command. He met with Rodes, Ewell, and Early and proposed that Ewell attack Culp's Hill the next day. Early opposed the plan. Lee suggested that the corps be withdrawn from town to shorten the Confederate Army's long constraining line. Once again Early disagreed, stating that the men's morale would suffer. Frustrated by his commanders' timorousness, Lee returned to his command post with no firm plans for the following day's action. Although unhappy about the advent of the battle, Lee surmised that it was unavoidable, given the circumstances. He summed up the day's events thus: "Encouraged by the successful issue of the engagement of the first day, and in view of the valuable results that would ensue from the defeat of the army of Gen. Meade, it was thought advisable to renew the attack."

At the end of the first day, Lee was a victor without victory firmly in his grasp, and Meade's defeat had forced the Union Army to withdraw and re-form at the best natural fortress in the vicinity.

Ewell lost his leg, and with it, his confidence. By failing to follow up the Confederate initiative on July 1st, he allowed Howard to consolidate south of town, thus creating the famous fishhook on Culp's Hill, Cemetery Hill, and Cemetery Ridge.

DAY TWO

Night lay heavy upon the land and dawn was hours distant when Meade arrived on Cemetery Hill. Reports had over 8,500 Union troops dead or missing – over a quarter of his army. Meade's officers hurried to remind him that the Confederates had lost a number of troops too. The difference, Meade knew, was that although the Confederates had suffered casualties, they had not been beaten off McPherson Ridge and driven off Barlow's Knoll, and they had not retreated at full speed through the town of Gettysburg with the enemy in hot pursuit.

Still, things were not totally lost. Buford had delayed the Southern advance, and Reynolds and Howard had kept the Southerners from occupying strategic points while the remainder of the Army of the Potomac coalesced there. By 0700 hours on 2 July all his army was in position except for VI Corps, one artillery brigade, and two mounted units. Although he did not know it, Meade had more troops present than Lee!

The Union Army, though driven back in retreat, had occupied the natural fortress provided by Culp's Hill and Cemetery Hill, with the nearby ridges connecting them to Little Round Top. The fishhook defense was already manned and taking on its classic shape. Hancock and Howard assured Meade that there was no finer place to fight a

The summit of Little Round Top had been cleared of timber, and it had not grown back. This bald spot provided an excellent artillery park which commanded the town, Devil's Den, Cemetery Ridge and Cemetery Hill. Had the South won this spot, they probably would have won the battle.

defensive action than the high ground which the Union Army held, and after a quick investigation, he had to agree.

The fishhook's tip was Culp's Hill (elevation 140ft), where the right flank was fixed. The Union defences curved a little over a half-mile northwest to Cemetery Hill (elevation 80ft) before straightening into a shank (elevation 40ft) formed by Cemetery Ridge, which extended south from Cemetery Hill to the base of Little Round Top (elevation 170ft). A shallow saddle 80ft high ran between Little Round Top and its southern companion, Big Round Top (elevation 300ft). A quarter-mile west and parallel to the fishhook's shank ran Seminary Ridge. Between Seminary and Cemetery ridges was the valley harboring the Wheat Field, Devil's Den, and the Peach Orchard, and down its center ran the Emmitsburg Road, which divided the valley into near-equal halves.

Meade made his headquarters in the Leister farmhouse at the eastern foot of Cemetery Ridge. Meade and Howard studied the disposition of their troops and mapped their placement in the early dawn. At Culp's Hill, XII Corps dug in. Between Culp's Hill and Cemetery Hill I Corps waited, and Howard's XI Corps held Cemetery Hill. From Cemetery Ridge to the base of Little Round Top both II Corps and III Corps formed a line facing west. Meade held V Corps in reserve at Powers Hill, a low rise just west of the Baltimore Pike and equidistant from every Union position. He hoped VI Corps would arrive shortly on that road, and from the way his troops were positioned, he could meet any challenge Lee threw at his army.

Late on the night of 1 July Lee had listened to a late caller – Ewell – who had outlined a plan to attack Culp's Hill which Ewell believed to be unoccupied. At first Lee agreed to the plan, but later that night, upon reflection, he realized that no Union commander would leave his back door unguarded, so Lee changed his orders and sent word to Ewell. That night Lee suffered from an intestinal malady. Since he still had not recovered fully from a horseback accident, and since the first stages of the heart disease which would later kill him had set in earlier that year, Lee was determined to exploit his army's situation to the fullest while he was still able. It was not often that the South had the Union Army at such a seemingly clear disadvantage, and using circumstances wisely, a bold general might end the war in this rural Pennsylvanian hamlet.

At 0530 on 2 July Lee met with Longstreet, Hood, Hill, and Heth on Seminary Ridge. Alternately studying a map and observing the distant Union left flank situated at the base of Little Round Top, Lee presented his plan of attack, which called for an assault on the Union left flank by Longstreet's divisions. As always, Longstreet was whittling while they discussed the plan of battle, but upon hearing Lee's order to attack the flank, Longstreet stopped whittling to disagree. Lee listened carefully to Longstreet's objections and then re-stated his orders: two of Longstreet's divisions, Hood's and McLaws', would attack the Union left.

McLaws joined them at about 0800 hours. Lee outlined his plan for McLaws and then showed him where he wanted his division placed – perpendicular to the Emmitsburg Road and occupying the ground between both Round Tops and the road. Longstreet modified Lee's orders, realigning McLaws' units from the way Lee had told McLaws to place them, but Lee intervened. Drawing a line on the map with his finger between the road and the hills, he said, quietly but firmly to Longstreet and all present, "I wish it [the division] placed as I have told General McLaws."

The plan called for an attack moving from south to north to roll up the Union left flank, with Law and Robertson attacking the Union left, keeping in contact with the Emmitsburg Road, and working their way up it, rolling back the blue-clad troops to their front, supported by Alexander's artillery and with their flanks defended by Hood's men. If the attack was properly executed, the Union Army would crumble and retreat to Cemetery Ridge or further east.

Kershaw's men were involved in fighting on all three days, but never did they engage so heavily or fight so valiantly as they did at Rose Woods and the Wheat Field close to Devil's Den.

Lee sent Capt. S.R. Johnson of the Confederate Army's engineers to reconnoitre the Union flank; then he rode over to Ewell's headquarters. Lee gave Ewell discretionary orders: upon hearing Longstreet's guns, press the Union right flank and exploit any advantage. This two-fold attack would tear the Union defense in half. He waited for Ewell to voice any objections, but Ewell did not, and Lee rode back to Seminary Ridge, arriving around 1115 hours. Capt. Johnson had not returned, and Longstreet had not yet advanced.

Lee again ordered Longstreet to advance, but Longstreet requested a delay in the attack until Gen. Evander Law (one of Hood's brigade commanders) arrived. Impatient with the slow crawl at which his masterstroke was moving, Lee reluctantly acquiesced to Longstreet's wishes. About an hour later Hood's and McLaws' divisions started moving to their designated positions, nearly four hours after Lee had first ordered the attack.

Around 1300 hours the long-lost Gen. J.E.B. Stuart arrived. The normally genteel Lee saw Stuart, grew red in the face and made a gesture as if to hit him, but then dropped his hand, admonishing, "I have not heard a word from you for days, and you the eyes and ears of my army." Stuart replied, "I have brought you 125 wagons." Lee's answer was curt, "They are an impediment to me now." As soon as he had said this, Lee's attitude changed, as he realized that Stuart, though misguided, had tried to help the Confederacy with these badly needed supplies. His next words were compassionate: "We will not discuss this matter further. Help me fight these people." Despite his midday arrival, Stuart's men were tired and unfit for battle that day because of their running battle while protecting the captured wagons from Union cavalry, and it was not until the next day that Lee was able to put his cavalry to use.

Hood's assault

Lee's problems were not over yet. No one had thought to plot a route which would conceal the Confederate approach and keep their destination secret so Meade could not rush reinforcements to the threatened area. As the route of march stood, movements of the Southern Army would telegraph Lee's plan to any alert Union observer. Topping Herr's Ridge, not far from Black Horse Tavern and the Fairfield Road, Gen. Joseph B. Kershaw of McLaws' Division realized that his route of march would be visible to Union observers. He stopped the march and conferred with McLaws and Longstreet. Longstreet was irritated at the delay but ordered an about face and a new route of march. McLaws ordered his men to countermarch to where they had started and then follow a circuitous route to keep their movements hidden from Union observers and signal corpsmen. Because of this maneuvre, Hood, who had been in

RIGHT Colonel Hiram Berdan's 1st US Sharpshooters wore green uniforms and carried the Sharp's rifle. Their firing and subsequent withdrawal from the woods prompted Gen. Sickles into a foolish advance to occupy the high ground.

Daniel Sickles was a vain, headstrong, insubordinate man whose inability to follow orders led to the heavy Union losses in the Wheat Field. His decision to move to high ground exposed the Union flank and left the line unsupported.

the rear, found himself leading the column. This tardy maneuvre doubled the distance the divisions had to travel and delayed their arrival and disposition into attack formation until shortly after 1500 hours.

McLaws' units from left to right were Barksdale and Kershaw leading, with Wofford and Semmes behind. To McLaws' right were Hood's units. Robertson and Law led, and were followed by Anderson's and Benning's units.

Hood's four brigades formed in two lines from the Emmitsburg Road to Bushman's Ridge, heading northwest, while McLaws' units were similarly formed up to Hood's left flank on Warfield Ridge, effectively extending the Confederate line. From noon Col. E.P. Alexander had been waiting at this site for Hood and McLaws with three artillery battalions, since one of his sharp-eyed men had spotted a shortcut here which both Hood and McLaws had overlooked. Alexander's three battalions – 50 or more cannons – were almost hub to hub along the crest of Warfield Ridge, laid in and ready for the command to fire. Alexander posted Maj. M.W. Henry's 19-gun battalion on Hood's right to support that flank.

Upon arrival, McLaws was surprised to find Union troops in the fields before him because he had been informed that there were no Yankees in this area. "The enemy was massed in my front and extended... as far as the eye could see." What he saw was Sickles' III Corps which had moved forward just prior to the Confederate arrival.

Earlier that day Maj.Gen. Daniel Sickles had worried about his III Corps' position at the low southerly end of Cemetery Ridge. The ground to his front looked higher, more defensible. When Sickles approached Meade about advancing, Meade refused to allow it, because such a move would put the entire Union line in jeopardy. Meade ordered Sickles to butt III Corps up against the left of II Corps and provide a continuous line. Sickles listened to his orders and then asked Meade if he could use his judgement in the disposition of his own corps, and Meade said that he could, provided he followed Meade's general plans. Sickles then left and found Henry Hunt and the two of them surveyed the ground to III Corps' front more closely. Sickles told Hunt he planned to occupy this ground. Hunt saw what the effect of moving Sickles' corps forward would do to the Union line, and told Sickles to await orders from command headquarters before he made any such move. Grudgingly Sickles held his ground, studying the seemingly better high ground before him, noting that with the withdrawal of Buford's cavalry his left was now exposed. Earlier, a hundred men of Berdan's Sharpshooters had been detached to keep an eye on the woods to Sickles' left, and for the last two hours he had heard the intermittent crackle of rifle fire from that direction.

At 1400 hours word came from the detachment of 1st and 2nd U.S. Sharpshooters that three columns of Confederate infantry were

moving east, evidently heading towards the exposed Union left flank. Sickles did not hesitate or send for instructions; instead he ordered the 11,000 men of his III Corps forward to the high ground. III Corps did not advance like skirmishers, or run like men charging onrushing enemies, they paraded forward with uncased colors waving, bugles blowing and a line of skirmishers to their front as if on parade or in dress rehearsal for a command review.

Sickles put Brig. J.J. Hobart Ward's men on the left, Col. Regis de Trobriand's men aligned in regimental columns to their right, in the Wheat Field, and Graham's men to their right, at a right angle to the Emmitsburg Road. Left to right Ward's units were: 4th Maine, 6th New Jersey, 40th New York (behind 4th Maine), 124th New York, 86th New York, 20th Indiana, 99th Pennsylvania, 115th Pennsylvania, and 8th New Jersey. In the Wheat Field, to Ward's right, left to right, de Trobriand's men were: 17th Maine, 5th Michigan, 110th Pennsylvania, 3rd Michigan, and 68th Pennsylvania. At a right angle to Graham's men, left to right, were: 114th Pennsylvania, 57th Pennsylvania, and 105th Pennsylvania; and the 63rd Pennsylvania were west of the Peach Orchard.

Birney's headquarters was on the north side of a small stone wall lining a lane near the Trostle farmhouse. Birney's brigades were deployed in an area strewn with massive boulders nearly 500 yards west and south of Little Round Top. This jumbled mass of house-sized rocks, orchards, and fields was known as Devil's Den. Sickles' men were in position by 1530 hours.

Sickles' 2nd Division, under Humphreys, advanced. Brig. Joseph Carr's brigade was placed to Graham's right, and their units formed a salient at the Peach Orchard. Brewster and Burling's brigades were kept in reserve behind Humphreys' line, which ran parallel to the Emmitsburg Road. A few of the five Union batteries nearby were engaged in a fitful artillery duel with Alexander's batteries while Humphreys advanced, but despite this, his brigade was deployed by 1600 hours.

About 1545 hours Meade rode to Cemetery Ridge's southern end to study his army's position. He reined his horse in sharply when he saw Sickles' position in the valley below, occupying the forbidden high ground, jutting out far ahead of the rest of the Union Army. He sent an aide down to III Corps summoning Sickles to him. Tight-lipped, Meade informed Sickles in no uncertain terms that his unauthorized advance was contrary to orders. Sickles realized from the tone of Meade's voice that he had gone beyond the pale, and so he offered to withdraw his men to their former position.

LEE DECIDES THE CONFEDERATE PLAN OF ATTACK, 2 JULY
Early in the morning of 2 July, 1863, Lee met with Hill, Longstreet, Heth, and Hood to consider his plan to advance north up the Emmitsburg Road and roll up the Union line from Little Round Top to Cemetery Ridge. It was a casual meeting, and Longstreet and Hood whittled to while away the time as Lee explained his plan. Because of problems, including a circuitous counter-march to avoid detection, the attack was delayed eight hours and resulted in the carnage of the Wheat Field and Devil's Den.

ABOVE **Birney's division of Hancock's corps occupied the salient at the Peach Orchard and bore the brunt of the Confederate assault on the area. Despite valiant efforts, they would have been overwhelmed had not reinforcements arrived.**

From a nearby ridge, Hancock and Gibbon watched the spectacle unfold. Gibbon, clearly anxious to join the coming fray and having seen Sickles' men advance, wanted to know if Hancock had received the order to advance. Hancock said that he had not. Studying the scene below and the surge of Confederates moving toward the newly emplaced Union line, Hancock told Gibbon, "Wait a moment and you'll see them come tumbling back."

At 1600 hours Hood's and McLaws' men were ready for the assault, and the general artillery barrage began in earnest, signalling the beginning of the attack Lee had ordered eight hours earlier. Under the canopy of artillery fire provided by Alexander's batteries, Law's and Robertson's brigades moved into the fields, under fire from skirmishers and the 4th New York artillery.

From the beginning, the Confederate battle plan went astray. Hood did not like the approach up the Emmitsburg Road, for there were too many places Union troops could fortify and blast his men to flinders. He sent word to Longstreet asking him if he could swing south and attack Big Round Top and the Union line from the flank and rear. Longstreet's reply was terse: "General Lee's orders are to attack up the Emmitsburg Road." Twice more Hood protested, but Longstreet was adamant, reminding Hood on the third request, "We must obey the orders of General Lee."

Hood nodded grimly. Then he gave his own orders. His men would not go up the lane like sheep to the slaughter; he ordered them to angle slightly east of the road and then go north. Law angled east, despite Hood's order for him to press northward. Robertson followed, staying in contact as best he could with Law, but in doing so, leaving his left flank

Fighting in Devil's Den was fierce. Many Confederate Sharpshooters were positioned in here and they shot Union officers from their positions. In the fierce hand-to-hand fighting that ensued, many were left in the jumble of boulders where they fell.

open and moving away from the Emmitsburg Road. They headed directly into Devil's Den. Because of slow communications or confusion, Hood's men would be fighting for an hour and a half before the remainder of the Confederate force was committed to battle.

Just after 1615 hours Hood reeled in the saddle his arm gushing blood, and he turned command over to Law. The latter knew the plans were unravelling, but didn't have the ability to stop them as his Alabamians surged toward the lower reaches of Big Round Top. Robertson moved his men toward Houck's Ridge.

Ward's men fired volley after volley into the approaching Confederates, and the 4th New York loaded canister. Time and again the Southerners moved forward, only to be slapped by canister and musketry until they stumbled backward; yet still they shook themselves, straightened their shoulders and charged again. Each time the charge came a little closer to the Union gunners and the kneeling infantry. At one point, the 1st Texas charged until they were within 140 ft of the line; then the 124th New York stood and fired en masse. The volley tore holes in the attack and seemed to "paralyze the whole line." Men began slipping from tree to tree, finding cover in shallow draws and behind boulders, firing at will and trying to close the distance between the gray and the blue lines. Later one Texan wrote that Devil's Den was more like "Indian fighting than anything I experienced during the war." Gradually the canister and determined volleys from behind stone walls and hastily prepared positions turned the day and the Confederates were forced back.

LEFT **Big Round Top, as seen looking south across the saddle from Little Round Top, is where Gen. Gouvenor K. Warren had artillery fire called in and saw hundreds of gleaming Southern bayonets massed underneath the trees preparing to assault.**

The fight for Little Round Top

South of Houck's Ridge, in the low spot between Devil's Den and the base of Big Round Top, the 44th Alabama charged into battle. They were shredded by a volley from the 4th Maine, but kept coming and blasted the reloading Yankees with a return volley. One Union soldier later commented that the line was "alive with burning powder." The ensuing firefight lasted 20 minutes, with neither side giving nor gaining ground until a quarter of the 44th was down. The Federals retreated deeper into Devil's Den as the 48th Alabama came to the 44th's aid. The 4th and 5th Texas joined the 4th Alabama and advanced on the western slope of Little Round Top.

Colonel William Oates' 15th Alabama climbed the steep slope of Big Round Top, pulling themselves up by holding bushes and branches while under constant fire to attack the understrength 2nd U.S. Sharpshooter detachment, easily displacing it. Oates' men were winded, and they stopped at the crest to catch their breath. Oates remembered the moment when he looked from this height (about 305ft) and surveyed the scene below and north of him. Big Round Top commanded the Union line. A few artillery pieces here could control the entire area.

Law sent Oates word that he was to take his men to the smaller hill north of them, Little Round Top. The saddle was 500 yards across, and on the opposite summit, all Oates could see was a small group of Union signal corpsmen frantically sending their signals. Further north he could see the Federal line digging in, but Little Round Top was virtually barren of troops. For the rest of his life, Oates felt that he had held the key to Gettysburg in his hands at that moment, but to his dismay there was no artillery with him. At his command, the 15th Alabama moved down the slope and joined the 47th Alabama to cross the saddle and occupy the smaller hill (Little Round Top) to their north. In the saddle, the 4th and 5th Texas joined them. Without hesitation, the Alabamians moved forward, intent on turning the Union flank – and no Union soldier was within sight.

Brigadier-general Gouvenor K. Warren was chief engineer to the Army of the Potomac. Earlier, while watching the progression of the Confederate battle plan from Little Round Top, he had realized what the thrust of the 4th and 5th Texas meant to the Union defense. He requested that a few artillery rounds from the 4th New York be directed at the woods on the larger hill. When the shells struck, Warren noted movement and glistening gun barrels – Confederates were massing there and would no doubt take this position unless something was done quickly. Warren realized that Little Round Top overlooked the entire Union line, and that whoever commanded its heights commanded the field of battle. Sending Meade a request for reinforcements, Warren waited impatiently for help. He saw Gen. George Sykes' V Corps approaching and rode down to tell Sykes he feared an impending Confederate assault. Sykes was riding at the head of Barnes' Brigade, but Barnes was riding elsewhere in the line. When an aide asked Col. Strong Vincent where Barnes was, adding that Sykes wanted a brigade placed at

Just above Chamberlain's 20th Maine's position, this looks south across the saddle where Oates' Alabamians and Texans assaulted the crude and hasty Federal breastworks constructed from deadfall and loose boulders.

ABOVE **General Gouvenor K. Warren saw the opportunity laying at the South's feet with Little Round Top unprotected. He saw that it was defended, and these are the commanders who helped hold the hill.**

the crest of the nearby hill to deter a Confederate advance, Vincent immediately gave his bugler the order to sound the charge, pulled his sword, and led his four regiments up the western slope at the double to occupy the hilltop.

As Vincent neared the crest, Confederate artillery opened up on Little Round Top, and he hastily deployed his units. To discourage a flank attack, Vincent placed Chamberlain's 20th Maine on the southern face, and on the western slope, to the 20th's right, he positioned the 83rd Pennsylvania, 44th New York and 16th Michigan. Using deadfall and loose rocks, the soldiers hastily formed crude, knee-high breastworks. They had barely knelt down when Chamberlain saw Southerners charging across the saddle between the Round Tops, heading north toward Little Round Top and from the west. The Union line was threatened from two sides!

Assessing his predicament, Chamberlain shifted four companies to the left, at a right angle to his line, forming a salient as Sickles had, but Chamberlain's salient curled around the crest of the hill like sharkskin on the hilt of a saber. Urging his men to wait until they were sure of their targets, he let the Confederates approach and then gave the command to fire when the Alabamians and Texans were less than 50 paces away. The volley crackled down the line, splintering the Alabamians' right flank and driving them downhill, away from the 20th Maine. After a minute the Alabamians regrouped and, uttering fierce battle-cries, charged the 20th Maine, using trees, rocks, and brush for cover as they fired, darted to a new position, reloaded, and fired again. The Alabamians drew so close that Union and Confederate soldiers were locked in a maelstrom of bayonets, clubbed rifles, and point-blank rifle fire. Chamberlain later said of the encounter: "The edge of conflict

General John Sedgewick (affectionately called "Uncle John" by his troops) arrived on the second day. His men were a much needed reserve. When asked by Meade if the army should stay or go, he said to stay and fight.

swayed to and fro, with wild whirlpools and eddies." Although outnumbered, the men from Maine had the high ground and some meagre fortifications. Their steady volleys and fierce fighting finally shoved the Confederates downhill toward the saddle.

Realizing that his men were down to their last couple of rounds, Chamberlain stepped to the front, drew his sword and crossed the breastworks, shouting "Bayonet!" The men of the 20th Maine were surprised by Chamberlain's sudden and seemingly impulsive action. Some advanced immediately and others were galvanized into action only after they saw their fellow soldiers surge forward. The leftmost wing had taken the initiative to advance, and led the way downhill, swinging from south to west as they pushed the battle-weary Confederates before them, moving en masse like a "great gate upon a post." This surprise bayonet charge broke the weary Alabamians who retreated across the saddle and up to the relative safety of Big Round Top's heights before the advancing men from Maine.

While this was going on, the 16th Michigan (to Vincent's right) was being pounded by the 4th and 5th Texas and was giving ground. Vincent went to rally them and was shot down. Falling, he cried, "Don't give an inch!" Warren was still seeking reinforcements for his impromptu command on Little Round Top. Finding 1st Lt. Charles Hazlett's Battery D, 5th United States Artillery, he sent them to the crest of the hill and

The tattered guidon of Battery D, 5th United States Artillery (red over white), 1st Lt. Charles Hazlett's battery, which kept the Confederates off the summit. Hazlett was killed when he bent over to hear the last request of a mortally wounded friend.

then left in search of more reinforcements. Upon their arrival, Battery D began shelling the oncoming Confederates; in turn, Southern snipers in Devil's Den began shooting at the artillerymen.

Locating Col. Patrick O'Rorke's 140th New York of Gen. Steven Weed's 3rd Brigade (V Corps), Warren ordered them up the hill. When O'Rorke protested, Warren yelled that he would take responsibility for O'Rorke's change of assignment. O'Rorke agreed and Warren left in search of Weed. The 140th charged up the hill, over the crest, and down into Robertson's Texans, blunting the Southern advance. O'Rorke was killed while leading the charge.

Finally, Warren located Weed, who agreed to take his remaining men to Little Round Top. Upon arrival, Weed learned from Hazlett that the battle was almost ended. As Weed turned to give his men orders, a sniper bullet hit him, passing through one shoulder, his spine, and exiting through the other shoulder. He fell, crying, "I am cut in two. I want to see Hazlett." As Hazlett was bending over to hear Weed's last request, a sniper bullet hit his head, killing him instantly.

20TH MAINE'S STAND ON LITTLE ROUND TOP, 2 JULY
Against several Southern wave attacks of Oates' combined Alabamians and Texans, Chamberlain's 20th Maine held the Union left flank on Little Round Top until they were almost out of ammunition. Fearing another wave attack if the Southerners regrouped, Chamberlain led his men downhill in a bayonet charge which thoroughly routed the now disorganized Southern troops.

Gen. Steven Weed was a friend of Charles Hazlett. On Little Round Top, Weed failed to stay under cover and a Confederate sniper shot him, shattering his spine, killing him.

The Peach Orchard and the Wheat Field

Even though Little Round Top was secure, the battle for Houck's Ridge and the Peach Orchard continued, with Benning's Brigade adding its strength to Law and Robertson against the Union line. Ward received reinforcements from de Trobriand's and Burling's brigades. With the addition of fresh troops and the movements of the first units in charge and countercharge, units became hopelessly entangled in the collapsing Union position.

The banks of Plum Run were lined with troops firing across the narrow slash of water, and the carnage was so great that this became known as the Valley of Death. Ultimately, remnants of the 1st Texas and three Georgia regiments overran the crest and seized three cannon guarded by the 99th Pennsylvania, which was overwhelmed. Birney's left flank was smashed, but at tremendous cost to both sides.

Anderson's five regiments of Georgians slammed against Birney's center in the Wheat Field, which was held by the rest of de Trobriand's men and Ward's right flank regiments. The Georgians pushed the Union troops out of the wheat only to have Sweitzer and Tilton from V Corps repulse them. The Georgians withdrew from the Wheat Field and re-formed in Rose Woods, south of the Wheat Field.

Kershaw and Semmes advanced across the fields of the Rose Farm, Kershaw leading and Semmes' brigade following. Union batteries, spotting their advance, opened fire, cutting 'great swaths' through the infantry. Once across the field, Kershaw joined Anderson's left southeast of the Peach Orchard, and overlapped Tilton and Sweitzer's line, threatening to flank them if they did not withdraw. Tilton withdrew into a stand of trees, but in doing so, exposed Sweitzer's flank. Barnes ordered the brigade back to the woods while a Union battery raked the Confederate left flank with canister.

Brigadier-general John Caldwell sent part of II Corps, under Col. Edward Cross, to bolster the Wheat Field, calling out to Cross, "This is the last time you'll fight without a star." Cross called back, "Too late, general, this is my last battle," having had a premonition of his own death. Cross moved his men diagonally across the Wheat Field from northeast to southwest. Anderson's and Kershaw's units were lined up at the woods with their rifles resting on the top rails of a fence, and to one Union soldier, those rifle barrels "glittered like a looking glass." The Confederates fired, and Cross was among those who fell. Another soldier recalled, 'Wheat flew in the air all over the field... cut off by the enemy's bullets.'

Colonel Patrick Kelly's 2nd Brigade came in fast to support Cross's flank, his men hammering the Southern ranks. These Irishmen had been absolved of sin by Father William Corby just prior to the battle, and they threw themselves into the fray like fearless dervishes. Reeling from Cross's and Kelly's attacks, Anderson and Kershaw were forced to withdraw when Zook's brigade hit them. The Southerners retired to Rose Woods. Semmes' Georgians and the 15th South Carolina moved forward and counter-attacked Brooke's brigade. After a quarter of an hour of vicious fighting, Brooke's men were forced back into the Wheat Field, but were saved from further defeat by Sweitzer's brigade, which stood fast to their right and helped stop the Southern counter-offensive.

OPPOSITE **G.T. Anderson's Georgians were crack troops, but Birney's men held the line in the Wheat Field and Peach Orchard against them. During this battle, Anderson was wounded.**

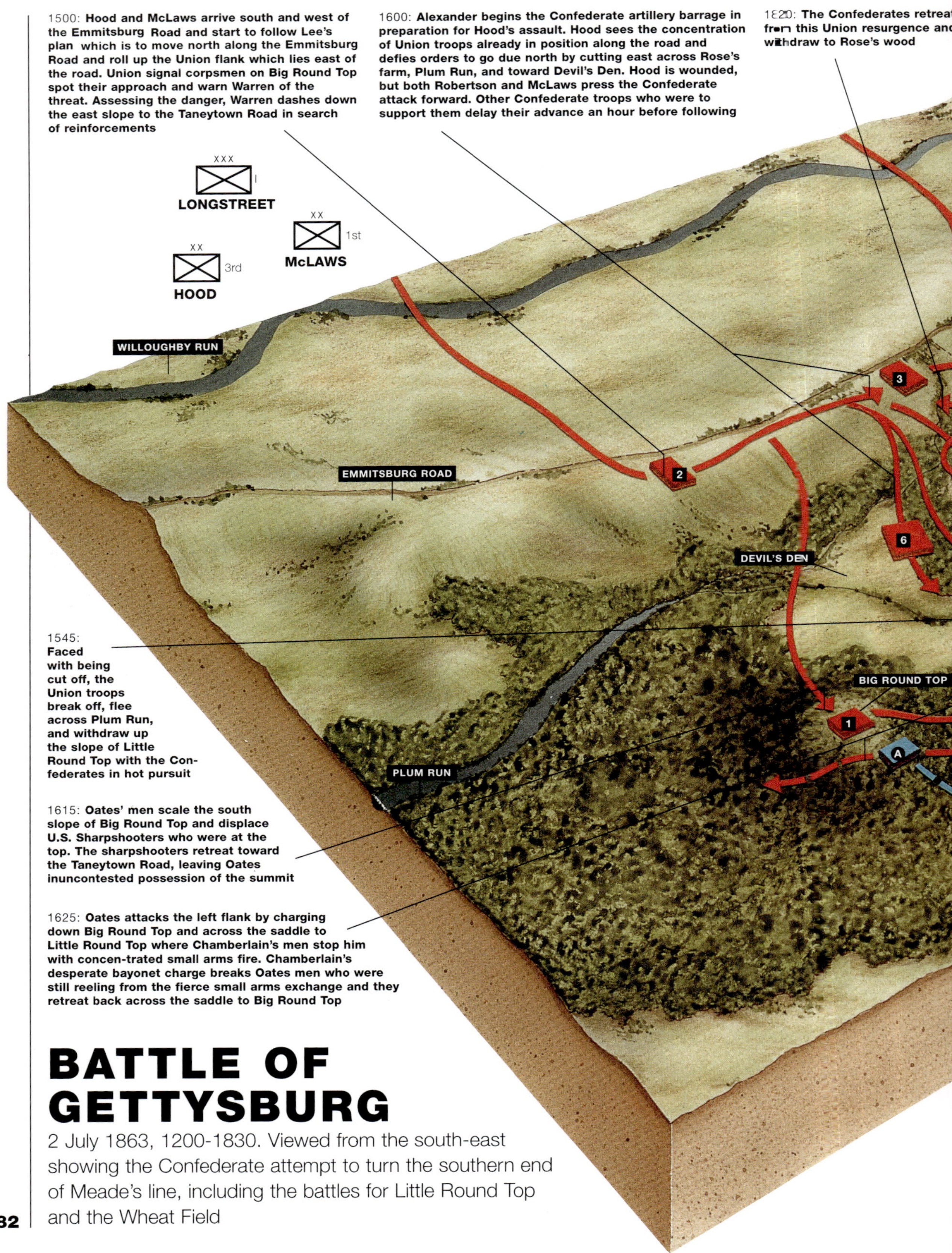

BATTLE OF GETTYSBURG

2 July 1863, 1200-1830. Viewed from the south-east showing the Confederate attempt to turn the southern end of Meade's line, including the battles for Little Round Top and the Wheat Field

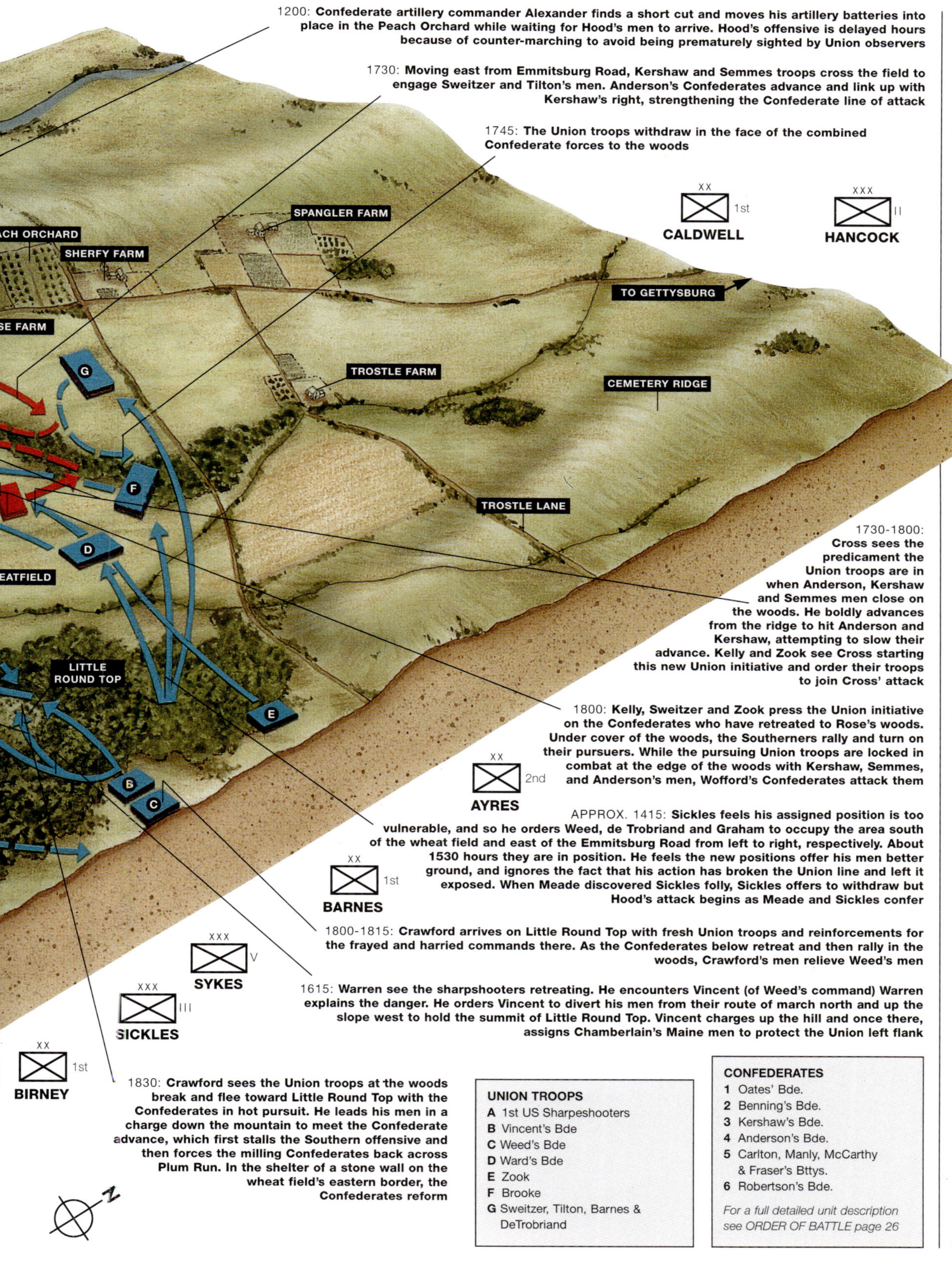
1200: Confederate artillery commander Alexander finds a short cut and moves his artillery batteries into place in the Peach Orchard while waiting for Hood's men to arrive. Hood's offensive is delayed hours because of counter-marching to avoid being prematurely sighted by Union observers
1730: Moving east from Emmitsburg Road, Kershaw and Semmes troops cross the field to engage Sweitzer and Tilton's men. Anderson's Confederates advance and link up with Kershaw's right, strengthening the Confederate line of attack
1745: The Union troops withdraw in the face of the combined Confederate forces to the woods
XX
1st
CALDWELL
XXX
II
HANCOCK
SPANGLER FARM
ACH ORCHARD
SHERFY FARM
TO GETTYSBURG
SE FARM
TROSTLE FARM
CEMETERY RIDGE
G
F
D
TROSTLE LANE
EATFIELD
1730-1800: Cross sees the predicament the Union troops are in when Anderson, Kershaw and Semmes men close on the woods. He boldly advances from the ridge to hit Anderson and Kershaw, attempting to slow their advance. Kelly and Zook see Cross starting this new Union initiative and order their troops to join Cross' attack
LITTLE ROUND TOP
E
1800: Kelly, Sweitzer and Zook press the Union initiative on the Confederates who have retreated to Rose's woods. Under cover of the woods, the Southerners rally and turn on their pursuers. While the pursuing Union troops are locked in combat at the edge of the woods with Kershaw, Semmes, and Anderson's men, Wofford's Confederates attack them
XX
2nd
AYRES
B
C
APPROX. 1415: Sickles feels his assigned position is too vulnerable, and so he orders Weed, de Trobriand and Graham to occupy the area south of the wheat field and east of the Emmitsburg Road from left to right, respectively. About 1530 hours they are in position. He feels the new positions offer his men better ground, and ignores the fact that his action has broken the Union line and left it exposed. When Meade discovered Sickles folly, Sickles offers to withdraw but Hood's attack begins as Meade and Sickles confer
XX
1st
BARNES
1800-1815: Crawford arrives on Little Round Top with fresh Union troops and reinforcements for the frayed and harried commands there. As the Confederates below retreat and then rally in the woods, Crawford's men relieve Weed's men
XXX
V
SYKES
XXX
III
SICKLES
1615: Warren see the sharpshooters retreating. He encounters Vincent (of Weed's command) Warren explains the danger. He orders Vincent to divert his men from their route of march north and up the slope west to hold the summit of Little Round Top. Vincent charges up the hill and once there, assigns Chamberlain's Maine men to protect the Union left flank
XX
1st
BIRNEY
1830: Crawford sees the Union troops at the woods break and flee toward Little Round Top with the Confederates in hot pursuit. He leads his men in a charge down the mountain to meet the Confederate advance, which first stalls the Southern offensive and then forces the milling Confederates back across Plum Run. In the shelter of a stone wall on the wheat field's eastern border, the Confederates reform
N
UNION TROOPS
A 1st US Sharpeshooters
B Vincent's Bde
C Weed's Bde
D Ward's Bde
E Zook
F Brooke
G Sweitzer, Tilton, Barnes & DeTrobriand
CONFEDERATES
1 Oates' Bde.
2 Benning's Bde.
3 Kershaw's Bde.
4 Anderson's Bde.
5 Carlton, Manly, McCarthy & Fraser's Bttys.
6 Robertson's Bde.
For a full detailed unit description see ORDER OF BATTLE page 26

General Crawford led V Corps' charge down Little Round Top's western slope, stopping the Southern advance and forcing the Confederates away from Little Round Top and back across the Wheat Field.

Near Rose Woods, just by the Sherfy Farm, the 57th and 114th Pennsylvania were crossing a road when Barksdale's Mississippians (who had just been ordered forward) attacked their flank, obliterating them and then moving forward to attack the 141st Pennsylvania at the Wentz Farm. The sudden attack cost the Pennsylvanians nearly three quarters of their unit, and the 21st Mississippi overran the point of the Peach Orchard salient and routed the 68th Pennsylvania. North of the angle, the 105th Pennsylvania was under relentless attack and crumbled.

Wofford's Alabamians and the 21st Mississippi surged to their right, along the Fairfield crossing, while Kershaw's, Semmes', and Anderson's units swept toward them – two converging Confederate arms. Kelly's, Sweitzer's, and Zook's brigades barely escaped the jaws of this trap and scrambled across Plum Gorge to Little Round Top with Confederates pursuing them almost to the base of the hill.

Crawford's Pennsylvanians now held Little Round Top. They moved aside to let the routed Federals pass safely through their lines and then closed ranks. After the last of the retreating Union troops had moved through, Crawford purposefully took the standard and led his men downhill toward the pursuing Confederates. On the way down, the Pennsylvanians blasted the Confederates with two massive volleys before charging into the now-disorganized Southerners, who retreated to the shelter of a stone wall which ran along the Wheat Field's eastern border.

North of the Wheat Field, Barksdale's and Anderson's men flowed across the flat toward Cemetery Ridge. In accordance with Lee's orders, Barksdale's men went forward in waves: Wilcox's Alabamians with Lang's Floridians on the left flank. They concentrated on Humphreys' Union

Brigadier Carnot Posey was supposed to support Wright's attack, but whereas Wright succeeded in reaching Cemetery Hill, Posey's men did not get beyond the Emmitsburg Road.

brigade, which was supported by Battery K of the 4th US Artillery and batteries F and K of the 3rd US Artillery. Through a storm of canister the Alabamians and Floridians moved steadily forward.

Barksdale swung through the Peach Orchard, pinning Carr's regiments in close combat. There seemed to be no co-ordination of Union action, and each command had to fend for itself. Battery K, 4th US Artillery, withdrew, and the 11th New Jersey took its place in the line near the Klingel house, only to be blasted by the Confederates. To the right of the 11th New Jersey, the 16th Massachusetts and batteries F and K, 3rd US Artillery, braced themselves for the onslaught. Wilcox's Confederates hammered them and then overran the position, capturing several cannon while the surviving infantry dispersed and withdrew piecemeal. North of the farmhouse, the 12th New Hampshire was savaged by the fire from Wilcox's Alabamians when they wheeled to face south, exposing their flank to them. Just north of the captured battery, the 11th Massachusetts turned south to face this threat, when a portion of Lang's brigade hit from the front and both sides. The survivors withdrew under heavy fire, taking casualties from both musketry and close combat mêlée.

Seeing Carr's line collapse, Col. William Brewster shifted six regiments of the New York Excelsior Brigade (III Corps, 2nd Division, 2nd Brigade) to face the onrushing Confederates. The 73rd New York, positioned west of Sherfy Farm, was slammed by the 13th and 17th Mississippi and was nearly engulfed, sustaining heavy casualties, but was not overrun. Birney ordered both brigades to retire. It was as orderly a withdrawal under fire as could be managed, with the experienced Union troops stopping no fewer than 20 times to volley at the onrushing Confederates.

General Ambrose Wright's Georgians were to the left of Wilcox's three Confederate brigades, and were moving directly toward the Codori farmhouse. Gibbon sent two II Corps regiments and Carr's final regiment to meet them. The Georgians drove them back and seized two cannon as they flowed back across the fields towards Cemetery Ridge. Gibbon rushed two more brigades forward. They slowed the Georgians only marginally, and were mauled in the process. In front of Cemetery Ridge and southward, splintered Yankees gave way before the seemingly invincible Southerners. At the Trostle Farm, the Confederate advance slowed as the 9th Massachusetts battery ripped holes in the gray-clad soldiers with load after load of canister. Captain Bigelow lost most of his horses and four of his six guns in the process, but his stand allowed the Union artillery reserve's 1st Volunteer Brigade to deploy on the ridge above and put down a wall of artillery fire to stop the oncoming Confederates. Alexander's Confederate artillery had unlimbered near the Emmitsburg Road and the Sherfy Farm and returned effective counter-battery fire.

Hancock saves the day

General Winfield Scott Hancock watched the Union line waver, break and then collapse piecemeal. He gathered units and thrust them forward. Among the first were Colville's 1st Minnesota, which charged Wilcox's Alabamians. The 1st Minnesota charged down the slope and crashed into the Southerners, being shot to pieces in the process. When the smoke cleared, only 38 men, led by a captain, remained from the 262 who had started down the hill (an 82% casualty rate), the largest proportionate loss of any Union unit at Gettysburg. Like the 9th Massachusetts battery, their selfless heroism bought precious minutes for Hancock and the Union.

Hancock sent Col. Willard's brigade against the wall of rebels. The repeated charges first slowed and then stopped the Confederate advance.

General Winfield Scott Hancock was a professional soldier who always managed to wear a clean white shirt, and his calm demeanour on Cemetery Hill calmed and inspired confidence in Union troops.

Barksdale fell, mortally wounded, and the complexion of the battle changed. Brigadier-general Alexander Webb's Brigade stood fast and drove the Confederates back. Now the Southerners had advanced too far without substantial support, and the Union troops counter-attacked. Still stinging from having seen bluecoats flee before the seemingly relentless gray tide, the Union soldiers pressed the tired Confederates hard, driving them back to the Emmitsburg Road, recapturing several cannon and clusters of weary Confederates. The Confederates withdrew to Seminary Ridge to regroup, and the Union Army withdrew to Cemetery Ridge, confident it had stopped the advance for now. The sun still shone through the gunsmoke-clouded air. It was 1930 hours.

From the southeast of Gettysburg, at 1730 hours, Sedgwick's VI Corps had begun arriving after a 35-mile trek from their starting point near Manchester, Maryland. Although too late for battle today, they would be an invaluable resource for tomorrow's action. Northeast of Gettysburg at 1600 hours, an artillery barrage had commenced from Benner's Hill, throwing hundredweights of shells on Culp's Hill and Cemetery Hill. Maj. J.W. Latimer had kept the bombardment up for a little over two hours. Union batteries had fired in response, and during the ensuing artillery duel, Latimer fell.

Meade called his generals together and asked them if they should stay or leave on the third day. Slocum spoke for many when he said, "Stay and fight it out."

Culp's Hill

When the duel ended, at 1830 hours, Ewell ordered Edward Johnson's Division to assault Culp's Hill. As Johnson advanced, he detached a brigade to his left to skirmish with Union cavalry. The distance was farther than Ewell or Johnson had imagined, and by the time Johnson's men reached Culp's Hill, darkness was falling. Culp's Hill was held by Greene's brigade, XII Corps, and Robinson's men (I Corps). The face of the hill was covered with clusters of boulders and wooded patches. When Johnson's men started up, the northern face of the hill erupted in a blaze of musketry which illuminated the dusk. The Union had dug in and used their prepared positions to offset the Southerners' superiority in numbers.

Greene's men held the northeast slope and crest, and Robinson's men were dug-in to their left. Throughout the fight, Greene had runners bring the men in the trenches ammunition so they could pour continuous fire into the oncoming Confederates. With the darkness, rough ground, and incessant musketry, the Southern advance stalled, gaining only the lower slope. An exception was Steuart's brigade, which stumbled upon abandoned trenches on the right of the Union position, but without real support, they could not press their advantage, and they sent word back that they needed reinforcements. Brigadier-general James Walker was sent to aid them. Although fighting continued long after dark, it gradually diminished, and ended with each side falling into fitful cessation of fire under the blanket of night.

General Alpheus Williams returned from a meeting with Meade to discover his units on Culp's Hill under attack from Walker's Confederates.

In the pitch black of night, Col. Wladimir Kryzanowski sent two regiments against a combined attacking force of Louisiana Tiger Zouaves and Carolinians.

Meade called a meeting of his generals which lasted until nearly 2100 hours. When Alpheus Williams returned to XII Corps' position from the meeting, his staff informed him of Steuart's Confederates in the trenches to the west. Williams requested permission to attack from both Slocum and Meade and received it. The problem was, the Confederates were in solid trenches with log walls and were protected by a swampy marsh to their left (his right). Williams' strategy for unseating the Confederates was to start a bombardment on the trenches early in the morning of 3 July at 0430 hours, while it was still dark, to drive the Southerners out, or at least force them to keep their heads down while his troops moved into position. Williams had struck upon a successful strategy. While the Confederates had to bring men forward, he was able to relieve his troops with men from other commands; thus when the line troops were weary, rested men took up their positions to continue the rain of rifle fire into the encroaching Southerners.

Sixty-five percent of Union casualties occurred on the second day, including Gen. Samuel K. Zook and three other Union brigade commanders – Vincent, Weed, and Willard.

While Culp's Hill was being contested in the early evening, Early advanced two brigades against Cemetery Hill, under Hays and Avery. Rodes was to support them, but his troops were poorly positioned and required time to get to the front. Meanwhile, Hays' Louisianans and Avery's North Carolinians moved forward at about 1930 hours (just about the time the Confederates had been shoved back to Seminary Ridge). Opposing them were Von Gilsa's and Aldebert Ames' brigades, positioned behind a stone wall. As the Confederates began their advance, four Union batteries on the heights fired on them. Avery was mortally wounded.

Avery's men came up to the stone wall and executed a right oblique to bring more guns to bear on the wall, but in doing so they exposed their left and rear to Battery E, 5th Maine, on Steven's Knoll. Together with the 33rd Massachusetts, Battery E pulverized the rear ranks. Instead of faltering, the Confederates charged forward into Von Gilsa's and Hays' positions, and the Union infantry broke. Following them closely, the Southerners overran Battery I, 1st New York Light Artillery, and charged on toward batteries F and G, 1st Pennsylvania Artillery. Although they fought valiantly, using rammers and sponges as well as small arms, the Union artillerymen were overcome and soon the Confederates held the crest. They expected reinforcements from Rodes, but none had yet arrived.

Two of Col. Wladimir Kryzanowski's regiments charged the Southerners, followed by Coster's New York and Pennsylvania units. Hays' Louisiana Tigers and Avery's Carolinians met them and fought them to a standstill in the pitch black of night. Twice the Union came forward, and twice they were driven back. Finally Carroll's brigade hit the North Carolinians and displaced them. The Tigers then closed with Carroll's men. The 7th West Virginia came to Carroll's aid and the Tigers were forced back, retreating down the hill into the safety of night, wondering where their reinforcements were. Hays said that his men had escaped only because it was dark, and that in daylight their flight would have been a "horrible slaughter." Rodes was just moving into assault position when the remainder of Hays' and Avery's men reached him. Except for late-night fighting on Culp's Hill, day two of Gettysburg had ended.

Lee had tried to come at Culp's Hill and the Union right, and now the Union left and lower center, without a conclusive victory; in fact Confederate offensives had not attained their objectives. Essentially, both armies still held the ground they had at the end of the first day. Tomorrow, he would break the Union line.

DAY THREE

FINISHING THE FIGHT AT CULP'S HILL

Before dawn, Lee sought out Longstreet. The latter had spent the previous evening and most of the night formulating a bold swing around Union lines, flanking the fishhook from a sudden encircling movement of Big Round Top. Longstreet's orders were not the plan Lee had suggested, and he scrapped Longstreet's encircling movement for a frontal assault on the Union lines almost opposite his headquarters. A small grove of trees marked the focal point of this assault. Moreover, Lee was concerned that Pickett's fresh division was still

This photo shows the area of Culp's Hill where Steuart's infantry attack gained a foothold before being dislodged.

ACTION AT CULP'S HILL, 2 JULY, 1863

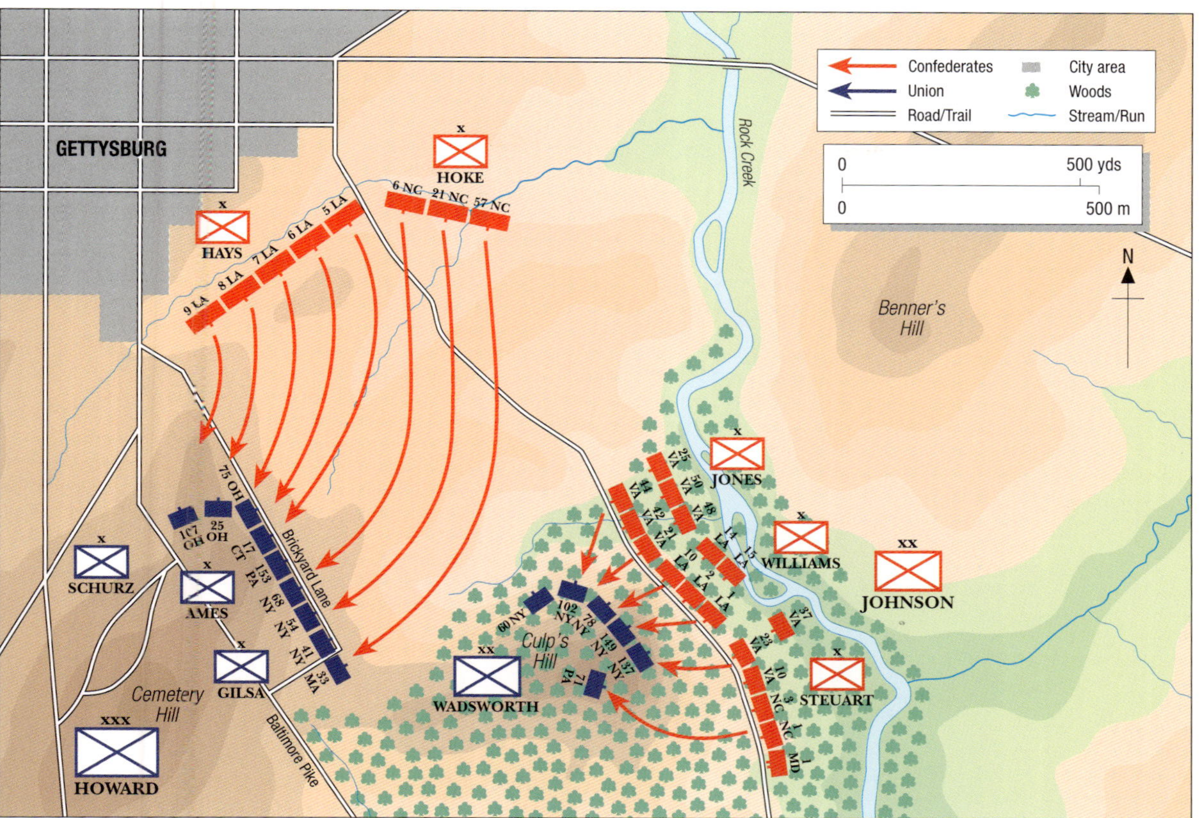

not on the front line. Lee thought his "incomparable" troops could crack the Union line, if anyone could. He planned an artillery assault to soften the Union line, and then the infantry would cross the distance of a little over a mile to close with the Union troops that remained. While all this was going on, J.E.B. Stuart's cavalry would swing wide of the battlefield, move north, and then cut down to harass the rear of the Union line from the east, completely smashing Union resistance. Longstreet studied the Union line through field glasses. "General," he said respectfully, "it is my opinion that no fifteen thousand men ever arranged for battle can take that position."

Lee selected Heth's and Pickett's divisions, four of Pender's brigades, and Wilcox's and Lang's brigades from Anderson. All units were battle-weary save Pickett's. Heth was not in command because of the head injury which had knocked him senseless for more than 24 hours. Pettigrew commanded, and he failed to inform Lee of the sorry condition of Heth's units. Still, Lee had faith in his infantry; had he known of the condition of Heth's command, he would have substituted another and stuck to his plan. Were this attack successful, Lee would break the back of the Army of the Potomac, and Lincoln would surely sue for peace.

Earlier, at 0445 hours on 3 July, 1863, the Union artillery barrage of the lower northern face of Culp's Hill had stopped, and before Williams could move his blue-clad men forward, Confederates who had slipped forward at night, under the command of Brigadier-general James Walker

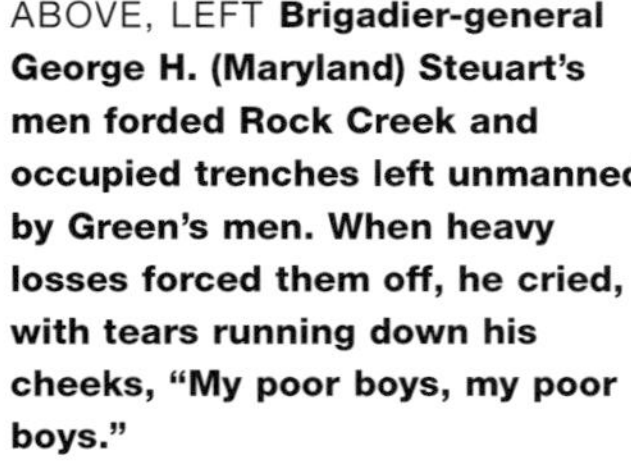

ABOVE, LEFT **Brigadier-general George H. (Maryland) Steuart's men forded Rock Creek and occupied trenches left unmanned by Green's men. When heavy losses forced them off, he cried, with tears running down his cheeks, "My poor boys, my poor boys."**

ABOVE, RIGHT **Brigadier Thomas H. Ruger's aide misunderstood his plans and sent the 2nd Massachusetts and 27th Indiana across an open meadow in a preview for the Union of what Pickett's men would face on a grander scale at Cemetery Ridge.**

(the Stonewall Brigade), stormed the slope to reinforce Steuart. The Confederate assault was supported by fire from units of Johnson's, O'Neal's, Daniel's and Smith's commands. Union Brig.Gen. John Geary's division held a position stretching from the crest of Culp's Hill, down the eastern slope and around to the Baltimore Pike.

Walker's brigade met Geary head-on, and Geary's division forced the Confederates back, while Confederates supporting Walker's brigade peppered the Union troops with small arms fire. In the battle that followed, the South attempted various and sundry sorties looking for a weak point in the Union line. The Union commanders shifted units back and forth between various positions so they could either reinforce their line or bring enfilading fire on the Southern thrusts. At 0800 hours O'Neal's Alabamians were pinned and withdrew slightly, holding their ground but now unable to advance. At 0900 hours Walker attempted to breach the line but was stopped. At 1010 hours Steuart and Daniel went forward, despite their protests that such an attack was doomed to failure. Canister and musketry shredded Steuart's command, and although Daniel did not suffer nearly the casualties Steuart did, his assault met with no success either.

At about 0945 hours Brig.Gen. Thomas Ruger ordered an attack on the breastworks near the northern meadow and Spangler's Spring. The plan called for skirmishers to attack, followed by a general assault by the 2nd Massachusetts and the 27th Indiana. An aide misunderstood the plan and passed the word to Col. Charles Mudge of the 2nd

Canister, the successor to grapeshot, consisted of four layers of seven balls on iron plates (with one usually missing from the top tier) which were fired from 12lb. guns, making them into massive shotguns.

Massachusetts that an assault against the breastworks had been ordered. Mudge was incredulous that such an order had been given. "It's murder," he said, "but it's the order. Forward, double quick."

Rifle fire along the Confederate position flamed, tearing holes in the advancing lines of Union infantry. Halfway across, the 27th Indiana faltered, stopped, and then began falling back. The 2nd Massachusetts forged ahead as four Confederate regiments blasted them with musketry. They made it to the breastworks, but Mudge was downed, and the incessant and accurate fire had left them at less than half strength. Then the 2nd Massachusetts fell back, retreating across the meadow. It was nearly 1145 hours.

On Seminary Ridge the Confederate units were massing for the attack in the tree-line. Pettigrew took the left, and his left flank was Brockenborough's Virginians. To Pettigrew's right Pickett formed his division in two parade-perfect lines, with Kemper's and Garnett's brigades in front and Lewis Armistead's unit in close support behind them. Lane's and Scales' brigades of Pender's command extended Armistead's line to the left and supported Pettigrew's brigades. Wilcox and Lang were east and south of Pickett in the fields, so they could guard the flank and rear of the attackers. In all, 50 regiments, comprised of soldiers from six states, would cross the fields to take the battle to the Yankees.

When the infantry was in place, E. Porter Alexander posted 75 guns from I Corps along the front in a 1,300 yard line from the Peach Orchard north to Spangler's Woods. Two Whitworths on Oak Hill would add their punch to this massive weight of artillery.

Longstreet was responsible for the assault. At 1145 hours, as the 2nd Massachusetts was withdrawing to Culp's Hill, Longstreet sent Alexander a note telling him that if the barrage failed to "drive off the enemy or greatly demoralize them," Alexander was to advise Pickett to abort the charge. The note worried Alexander, and he conferred with Brig.Gen. Ambrose Wright. The two sent Longstreet a note stating that if Longstreet had any alternative to the assault and bombardment he should consider it, for the Confederate artillery wagons were very low on shells and this barrage would virtually empty them. Longstreet read their note seriously, and then penned a response to Alexander a half hour later, telling him to select the proper moment to tell Pickett when to advance.

Brig. James L. Kemper commanded Pickett's brigade and as far as he knew, the Union troops and artillery had been subjected to intense artillery fire which had "softened them up."

Pickett's Charge

The assault on Culp's Hill was over. The noonday heat was sweltering, and soldiers of both sides waited with ready rifles, sweat streaming down their faces. At 1300 hours Longstreet sent Col. J.B. Walton the following order: "Colonel, let the batteries open [fire]."

Two minutes later a pair of cannon from the Washington artillery of

LEFT **Longstreet liked a defensive battle and thought Lee's order to attack the Union line was a mistake, but because Lee ordered it, he let Pickett lead the charge anyway.**

RIGHT **Ironically, the gatehouse of the cemetery on Cemetery Hill bore a sign warning that anyone discharging a weapon on the premises would be subject to prosecution.**

New Orleans signalled the commencement and Seminary Ridge exploded, as nearly 170 Confederate guns thundered and roared.

The target of the Confederate gunners was Cemetery Ridge, specifically a small grove of trees Lee had noted, making the Union soldiers lie flat. As one soldier said, "All we had to do was flatten out... and our empty stomachs did not prevent this." The Union was ready, and its artillery replied to the Confederate artillery. One soldier remembered, "The whole country around seemed to be in a blaze of gunpowder." Sadly, the Confederate guns shot long, destroying sixteen Union horses in the yard of Meade's HQ, and shelling Meade's headquarters on the eastern slope. Although the Confederate storm lasted a little over two hours, because the shots were long, Union troops on the western slope were relatively uninjured.

They were in a high state of readiness, waiting for the Confederate advance so they could give the Southern infantry a little of what the Southern artillery had been giving their rear ranks. The heaviest losses were Union artillerymen on the slope behind the waiting Union infantry. Losses of men and guns were small, compared to the amount of rounds fired, but horses and caissons took a lot of damage from artillery fire. A few batteries limbered and pulled out under the rain of Southern fire.

At 1450 hours Alexander saw the Union gun crews move out and he misread the situation. He believed the Union line was breaking under the stress of the Confederate artillery assault. He sent to Pickett, saying,

"For God's sake come quick. The 18 guns have gone. Come quick or my ammunition will not let me support you properly." The fate of nearly 15,000 Southerners rested on Alexander's note.

Pickett was waiting with Longstreet, watching the artillery assault on Cemetery Ridge, when Alexander's note arrived. Pickett read it quickly, and then handed it to Longstreet, asking, "Shall I advance?" Longstreet did not want this assault, and although Lee entrusted him to carry out its implementation, Longstreet believed the best offense was a good defense, and this assault was not a good defense. Furthermore, Longstreet liked Pickett, and had always looked out for him. To send Pickett forward into an uncertain assault against prepared and massed Union troops was the hardest order Longstreet would ever have to give. When Pickett handed him the note, Longstreet studied it with bowed head, and then turned to mount his horse without uttering a word. Pickett persisted, "I shall lead my division forward, sir?" Longstreet's nod was almost imperceptible, and words failed him. Pickett sprang to his saddle, gave a touch to the brim of his kepi, and galloped off to his command and an appointment with history.

ABOVE **Meade set up head-quarters in the Lister Farm on the east side of the hill where most of the Confederate rounds landed, killing many horses in the yard and coming close to wounding Meade himself.**

ABOVE, RIGHT **George Pickett was devoted to LaSalle Corbel of Lynchburg, and gave up strong drink because of love, but still he led his men into battle without thought of personal danger, saying, "Charge the enemy and remember Old Virginia."**

The Confederates waited in dressed ranks, Pickett's Virginians with Lang to their right and Wilcox to the extreme right. To their left were Thomas, Perrin, Ramseur, Iverson, and Doles. Kemper commanded Pickett's lead brigade. To his left was Garnett's brigade. Behind Garnett came Armistead. The men waited in the cover of the trees, lips set, sweat trickling down their backs.

Just after 1510 hours Pickett moved to the front of his men, turned in the saddle to face them and commanded, "Charge the enemy and remember Old Virginia." Facing the Union lines, his voice was loud and clear, "Forward! Guide center! March!" And with that the Southern advance began, rifles with fixed bayonets at low port resembling a "glittering forest of bayonets," 100–110 paces to the minute, blue flags fluttering in the slight breath of afternoon breeze, voices silent and faces determined, having been ordered neither to run nor to utter their famous rebel yell. In the late afternoon heat (it was the hottest part of the day – nearly 90 degrees Fahrenheit and very humid), the skirmishers stepped from the woods and started a sixteen and a half minute walk that led 10,000 Confederates forever into history.

On Cemetery Hill members of Hancock's II Corps, Gibbon's and Hays' divisions and two of Doubleday's brigades watched the eerily silent advance while crouched behind stone walls 30 inches high that ran underneath split rail fences. The fence line ran from Bryan's Farm south, turning in a right angle west, and then going down the ridge before continuing south. Six batteries supported the infantry.

Gibbon's men held the trees, and to their right were Hays' men four deep – seasoned fighters all. About 100 yards in front of this line, Federal skirmishers lay concealed in the grass, waiting for the Southern advance. Thirty-one guns were in the line. The distance between the Confederates and the Union line was a little over a mile, and was covered by artillery positioned on Little Round Top, Cemetery Hill and Cemetery Ridge. Advancing Confederates would be subjected to enfilading fire from in front and on both sides. As soon as Pettigrew's troops started forward from the tree-line, Union gunners began blasting them with everything they had. "The havoc... was truly surprising," one Union artillery officer commented. At first Pettigrew's men drew most of the fire, leaving Pickett's men relatively untouched. Pettigrew's line swerved because of the rain of shot and shell, and Pickett's men, already in parade-perfect ranks, did a 45-degree oblique to keep in sync with Pettigrew's advance, which was straying. When the Confederates reached the Emmitsburg Road, guns on Cemetery Ridge and Little Round Top opened fire.

At the ruins of the Bliss barn, Pickett stopped and dressed ranks before resuming the advance. Brockenborough's men, however, were unsteady and hesitated when the other Southerners started once more

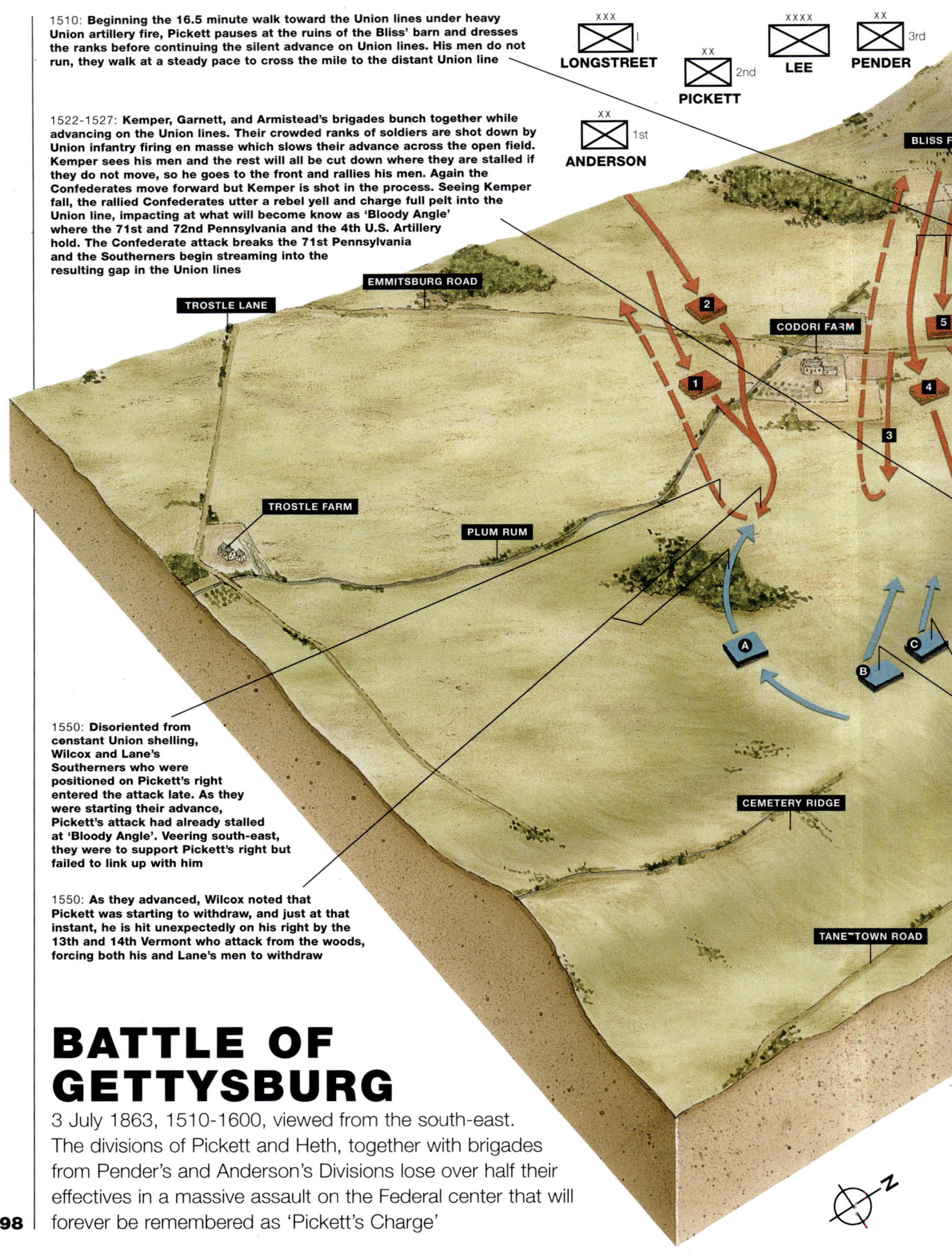

1510: **Beginning the 16.5 minute walk toward the Union lines under heavy Union artillery fire, Pickett pauses at the ruins of the Bliss' barn and dresses the ranks before continuing the silent advance on Union lines. His men do not run, they walk at a steady pace to cross the mile to the distant Union line**

1522-1527: **Kemper, Garnett, and Armistead's brigades bunch together while advancing on the Union lines. Their crowded ranks of soldiers are shot down by Union infantry firing en masse which slows their advance across the open field. Kemper sees his men and the rest will all be cut down where they are stalled if they do not move, so he goes to the front and rallies his men. Again the Confederates move forward but Kemper is shot in the process. Seeing Kemper fall, the rallied Confederates utter a rebel yell and charge full pelt into the Union line, impacting at what will become know as 'Bloody Angle' where the 71st and 72nd Pennsylvania and the 4th U.S. Artillery hold. The Confederate attack breaks the 71st Pennsylvania and the Southerners begin streaming into the resulting gap in the Union lines**

1550: **Disoriented from constant Union shelling, Wilcox and Lane's Southerners who were positioned on Pickett's right entered the attack late. As they were starting their advance, Pickett's attack had already stalled at 'Bloody Angle'. Veering south-east, they were to support Pickett's right but failed to link up with him**

1550: **As they advanced, Wilcox noted that Pickett was starting to withdraw, and just at that instant, he is hit unexpectedly on his right by the 13th and 14th Vermont who attack from the woods, forcing both his and Lane's men to withdraw**

BATTLE OF GETTYSBURG

3 July 1863, 1510-1600, viewed from the south-east. The divisions of Pickett and Heth, together with brigades from Pender's and Anderson's Divisions lose over half their effectives in a massive assault on the Federal center that will forever be remembered as 'Pickett's Charge'

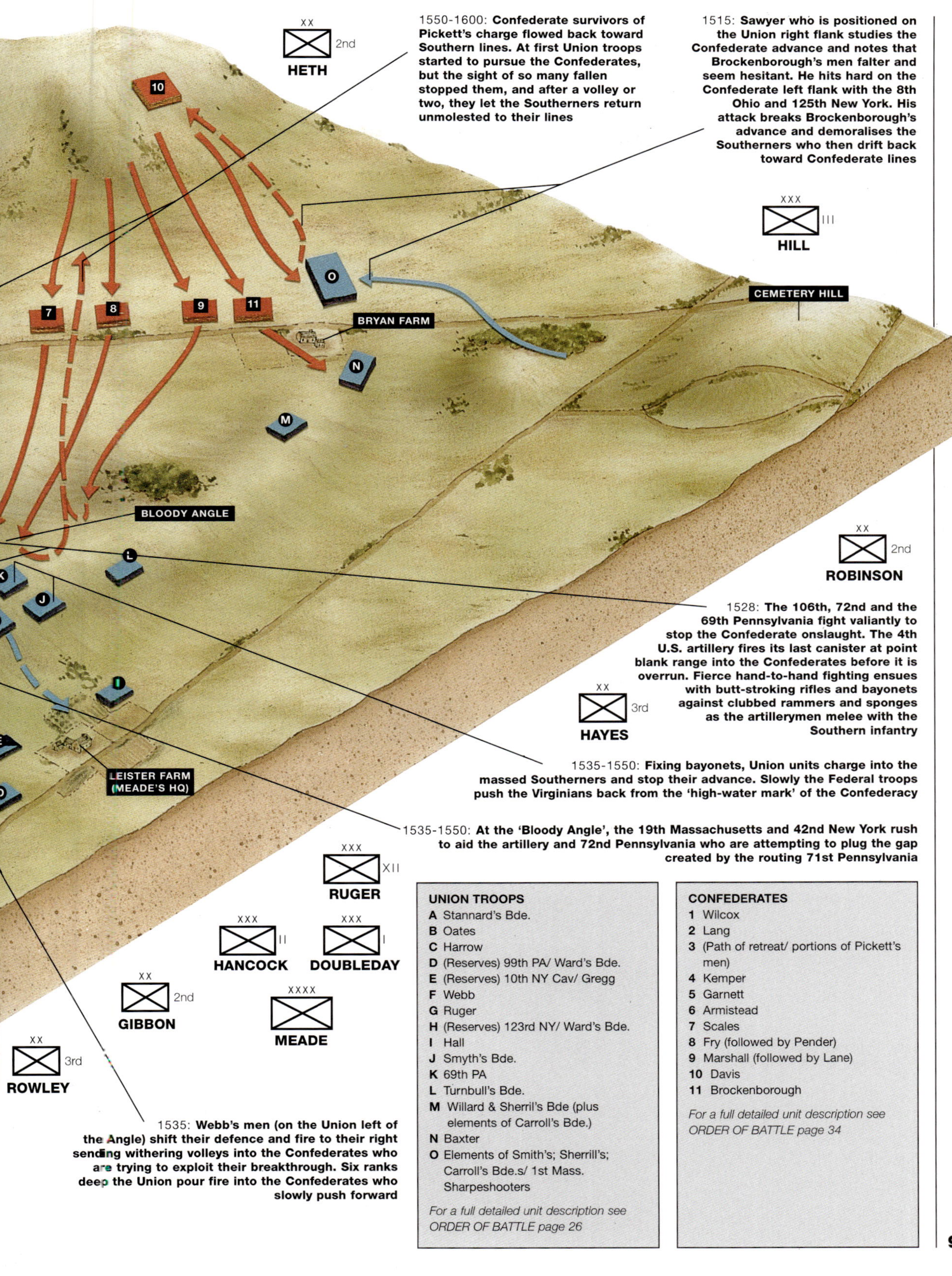

UNION TROOPS
- **A** Stannard's Bde.
- **B** Oates
- **C** Harrow
- **D** (Reserves) 99th PA/ Ward's Bde.
- **E** (Reserves) 10th NY Cav/ Gregg
- **F** Webb
- **G** Ruger
- **H** (Reserves) 123rd NY/ Ward's Bde.
- **I** Hall
- **J** Smyth's Bde.
- **K** 69th PA
- **L** Turnbull's Bde.
- **M** Willard & Sherril's Bde (plus elements of Carroll's Bde.)
- **N** Baxter
- **O** Elements of Smith's; Sherrill's; Carroll's Bde.s/ 1st Mass. Sharpeshooters

For a full detailed unit description see ORDER OF BATTLE page 26

CONFEDERATES
- **1** Wilcox
- **2** Lang
- **3** (Path of retreat/ portions of Pickett's men)
- **4** Kemper
- **5** Garnett
- **6** Armistead
- **7** Scales
- **8** Fry (followed by Pender)
- **9** Marshall (followed by Lane)
- **10** Davis
- **11** Brockenborough

For a full detailed unit description see ORDER OF BATTLE page 34

General Alexander Webb's headquarters area at Gettysburg. Webb is standing at the left, before his tent, in full uniform and boots.

toward the waiting Union line. Colonel Sawyer of the 8th Ohio and part of the 125th New York saw Brockenborough's hesitation and charged boldly into the uncertain Confederate infantry's flank, dissipating the Virginians.

When the Confederates neared, Union skirmishers stood and unleashed a couple of volleys before stepping back to the Union lines. At this point, Union line artillery fired canister almost into the faces of the advancing Confederates, tearing gaping holes in their lines. When Archer and Barnett closed within 250 yards of the Union position, Gibbon's men stood on command and calmly volleyed into the close-packed Confederates. Every member of the 1st Virginia's colour guard was knocked to the ground by small arms fire; the 8th Virginia's colours fell no fewer than four times in almost as many minutes. Hays had his men wait until Marshall's and Davis' brigades had begun moving over the rail fences on the west side of the Emmitsburg Road, and then he fired.

Confusion reigned in the Confederate advance. With the fire coming from all sides, the rear ranks pushed forward, and the lead units fell as though they had been poleaxed; a Confederate officer later described it as a "mingled mass from fifteen to thirty deep." Kemper's, Garnett's and Armistead's men pressed together. Trying to bring a semblance of order to the advance, Kemper went down, wounded. But before he fell, he galvanized the Southerners and they fired back. The act of firing seemed to break the spell, and the Confederate ranks surged forward, swarming the angled stretch of wall 1,000 yards below the Bryan barn. This stretch of wall would become infamous as the "Bloody Angle." Directly in their path was battery A, 4th US Artillery, supported by Webb's Philadelphia Brigade. Two units were in back of the line and a little way up the hill – the 72nd and the 106th Pennsylvania.

With the spell broken, the long-silent Confederates defiantly screamed their rebel yell, a long, eerie ululation, and raced forward to the wall. The 71st Pennsylvania broke. The artillery fired the last of the canister at point blank range, and suddenly the gunners were fighting tooth and nail, using handspikes and rammers against Confederate bayonets. To the 71st's left, the 69th Pennsylvania loaded and fired like automatons, but still the Confederates pressed forward. Suddenly volleys from uphill and the flanks sliced into the oncoming Confederates as the 72nd and 106th Pennsylvania opened fire to support the 69th.

Lewis Armistead waved his hat on his sword to show his men which way to go and to encourage their advance. He brought his men straight toward the two Pennsylvania units in the grove of trees. The Union troops volleyed and Armistead fell, his hat still perched on his sword. Some of Armistead's men made it to the grove of trees, but Union reinforcements were coming to the front. The 19th Massachusetts and the 42nd New York entered the trees and swept through the light woods, driving the rushing Confederates back. At less than ten paces the Union units exchanged fearsome volleys with the still-advancing gray line.

South of the trees, the 69th Pennsylvania was overrun by Southerners who pushed toward the 1st Battery New York Light Artillery. Gunners slammed canister down barrels and jerked lanyards, sending a hail of musket balls and shrapnel into the charging gray line. When the smoke cleared, none of the gray-clad attackers was still standing. The 26th North Carolina charged Hays' front. The 1st Rhode Island Light Artillery used double canister on them, and only a sergeant and an enlisted man made it to the safety of the wall. The North Carolinians and Mississippians retreated to Seminary Ridge.

At the Bloody Angle and the grove, Federal reinforcements began turning the day, slowly driving the Southerners out of the trees and back toward the wall. The 59th New York, 7th Michigan, and 20th Massachusetts joined the 69th Pennsylvania. Hancock rallied the 19th Massachusetts and the 42nd New York, shouting, "Forward men! Now's

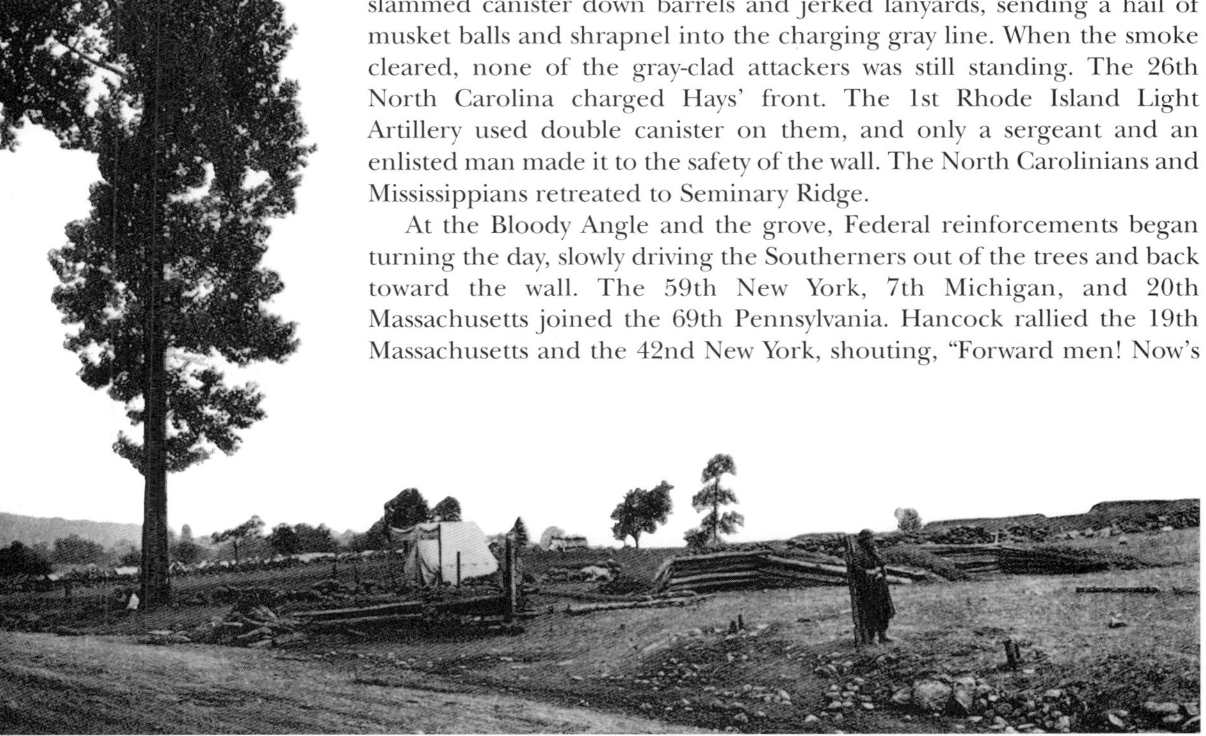

Bloody Angle salient was the focal point of Pickett's Charge. Here Union troops behind small stone walls were relatively untouched by the artillery barrage and awaited the inevitable Southern assault.

your chance!" Federal troops were in ranks six men deep, and they exchanged horrendous volleys at five paces with the Confederates. Near the clump of trees a Union bayonet charge slammed into the Virginians and they reeled backward. Men were locked in hand-to-hand combat, but this Union counter-charge had broken the back of the Southern assault and Pickett's men began retreating to their own lines.

Wilcox's and Lang's brigades entered the attack as Pickett's Virginians began their withdrawal from the Bloody Angle. Under constant shell-fire since leaving the protection of the trees, the confused soldiers had marched straight instead of filling in on Pickett's right flank. The 14th and 16th Vermont, under Stannard, charged the Confederates. The 2nd Florida, which was on Lang's left flank, saw Pickett retreating and surrendered almost to a man when the Vermonters charged. As

PICKETT'S CHARGE, 3 JULY

The epitome of the Confederate cavalier, gallant Gen. George Pickett, told his men, "Charge the enemy and remember Old Virginia!" With quiet desperation he watched his Virginian division march toward Cemetery Ridge. Five brigades of Confederates advanced at walking pace across virtually open fields upon hearing his order, and marched forever into the pages of history.

soon as Wilcox determined that Pickett had ordered the retreat and that this was not just a temporary push back by the Union, he ordered his troops to withdraw. It was just after 1600 hours.

Wilcox found Lee and reported the mauled condition of his brigade and their withdrawal. Lee's appearance was drawn, almost haggard. "Never mind, general," he told Wilcox, "all this has been my fault. It is I who have lost this fight, and you must help me out of it as best you can." This was a far cry from the commander who thought his men invincible. Seeing Pickett, Lee directed him to move his division behind (to the west of) the woods. "General Lee," Pickett replied, his voice low and almost cracking from the strain, "I have no division." Lee's tone was consoling: "The name of Virginia [is] as high today as it has ever been." Many have blamed Pickett for the charge, some point to Longstreet, but in the end,

the real blame lies with Robert E. Lee. He realized this and took the full responsibilty himself, saying, "My fault, my fault!"

The attack had been a complete disaster. Pettigrew and Trimble each lost more than half of their command, with Pickett overall losing 40% of his effectives. Three of his generals – Kemper, Armistead and Garnett – were either dead, dying, or severely wounded. Four regiments had lost more than 80% effectives. Of nearly 11,000 men who walked for sixteen and a half minutes across the field, just over half were dead or wounded. "We gained nothing but glory – and lost our bravest men." In all, the South lost nearly 6,500 dead, wounded, and captured.

The Union butcher's bill was perhaps 1,500 men – not as great numerically, nor percentage-wise. In a defensive mode, the Union had lost fewer troops; and in a battle of attrition, as Gettysburg was, seeing your enemy lose more men was what decided who was the victor. Hancock said, in a message to Meade, "I have never seen a more formidable attack." He then followed up with the comment that he felt Lee's army was broken and that the Union could end this war here and now by destroying the Army of Northern Virginia if Meade would just commit the V and VI Corps to a counter-attack.

Meade hesitated to order a counter-attack: Federal casualties were over 1,500 men – about a quarter of the troops who were at the Bloody Angle. His men had been savaged on all three days of the battle, and through shuttling troops from one position to another in the line, many units had become disorganized and were far from their supplies. His commanders had suffered: Gibbon was wounded and Hancock too, his life having been spared by his belt buckle when a bullet shattered the pommel of his saddle, sending splinters, bullet fragments, and a nail (probably from the pommel) into his thigh and stomach. The buckle deflected a piece of shrapnel that would have gutted him, and thus turned a virtually fatal stomach wound into a

Brigadier-general Alexander Hays' seasoned fighters stood in ranks four or more deep to pour withering fire into Pickett's Confederates who charged Cemetery Hill.

When the Confederates broke through the Bloody Angle and shook the 69th, Cowan's battery was at first masked. When the 69th moved, this kind of 'grapeshot' was fired at ten yards into the oncoming Southerners.

ABOVE **These are the men of Cowan's battery who served at Gettysburg. Their gun was masked by the 69th Pennsylvania, which fortuitously moved as the Confederates closed, allowing Cowan to give them a whiff of grape at little more than ten paces. Six months later, two artillerists, Sgt Uhlster (#A) and Corp. Tucker (#B) were crippled and killed respectively at Cedar Creek.**

BELOW **This photograph from June 1863 gives an idea of what Pickett's men faced. The scores of guns whose battery fire could come from the front and both sides as they advanced had to be silenced, but the Confederate artillery barrage to knock them out failed to do so.**

merely painful one; a hastily applied tourniquet staunched the blood from his thigh.

Psychologically the Union troops were no less battered than their Confederate counterparts, for waiting in a battle is as telling as attacking and for three days the Union Army had waited while Lee and his generals probed and prodded, seeking the weak spot in the Union's fishhook defence. Because of the interior arc of the fishhook and Meade's skilful shuffling of troops, the defense, the Army of the Potomac, and the Union itself remained intact.

Meade evaluated Hancock's request and in the end decided his troops were worn out, thus making such a counter-attack virtually impossible. To make certain Lee did not intend to attack again, Meade ordered a reconnaissance in force of the area by two brigades, one to see what the situation really was, and one to support them in case of trouble. The brigades got as far as the Wheat Field near the Emmitsburg Road and saw Confederates withdrawing to the west of the road (probably Law's and Hood's troops), and positioned themselves there to observe the continuing Southern withdrawal.

Meade called his commanders together for a meeting. In the meeting Pleasonton challenged Meade, saying, "General, I will give you half an hour to show yourself [to be] a great general. Order the army to advance, while I will take the cavalry and get in Lee's rear, and we will finish the campaign in a week." Of the commanders present, Hancock, Doubleday and Howard supported Pleasonton's somewhat rash suggestion. However, Pleasonton's cavalry had not been as badly mauled as most of the infantry, and was probably far more fit for combat than most of the units.

Meade was well known for his sudden, sharp bursts of temper, but on this occasion he either restrained himself or was too weary to fight with Pleasonton. He countered with a question: "How do you know Lee will not attack?" Before Pleasonton could continue, he finished, "We have done well enough." Pleasonton protested that Lee's army was shattered, far from supply, and low on ammunition. Meade did not reply directly to that, but requested that Pleasonton take a ride with him to view the battlefield. Meade was aware that it was one thing for an army in a defensive position to be victorious, and it was an entirely different matter for that same army to switch from a defensive to an offensive mode. He had learned that from studies of history – particularly Hastings.

CAVALRY ACTION AT LOTT'S FARM, 3 JULY
Although many cavalrymen rode to battle and then fought dismounted, on 3 July Brig.Gen. Wade Hampton and Brig.Gen. Fitzhugh Lee of J.E.B. Stuart's command charged Custer's Michigan cavalry head-on at Lott's Farm. Although the action was bloody and Hampton was wounded in the fray, it was indecisive and both sides withdrew. This engagement did, however, keep Stuart from harassing the Union rear while Pickett assaulted its front.

The cavalry actions at Gettysburg

To many, the battle of Gettysburg climaxes with the Bloody Angle, but the story continues, for east of this battlefield, a lesser-known cavalry engagement took place. Earlier in the day Stuart had been sent to swing around the Confederate left above the Union position and, at the proper moment, move down from the north and strike from the east to hit the Union Army from the rear and harry it. This was the crowning touch to Lee's plan, but with the collapse of Pickett's offensive, it was never to come to fruition

At almost the same time, but at the southern end of the battlefield, a Union cavalry offensive was mounted. At noon two Union cavalry brigades, under Farnsworth and Merritt, were sent to swing wide of the Union left flank and discourage any Confederate advances there. At about 1500 hours the Union cavalry encountered elements of Hood's and Law's men on the Union's extreme left flank (the Confederate right flank) and they skirmished for several hours without either side gaining any real advantage. The heavier firepower of the Confederates nullified the mobility of the Union cavalry.

Armistead, his hat on his sword as a visual guidon to his men, overran a cannon and then fell mortally wounded. Where he fell is generally considered the 'high water mark' of the Confederacy.

Around 1700 hours, Pleasonton felt Meade was going to counter-attack, so he ordered the Union cavalry forward against the Confederate line. Twice the Union cavalry was repulsed, and the third time Pleasonton ordered Farnsworth to lead the charge in person. Charging en echelon, the Union sliced through the Confederate infantry and to its rear, where Farnsworth's men turned and galloped back to their own line. In the process they captured nearly 100 Southerners but lost 60 men, including Farnsworth who was killed on the charge back to the Union lines. It was a spectacular cavalry charge, but it accomplished little, save to reinforce the notion that men like Pleasonton, Kilpatrick and Custer were the last hussar-like cavalrymen, and that Buford perhaps knew the true value and strength of cavalry.

General Richard Garnett, possibly still smarting under the allegations of cowardice Jackson had brought against him, was in the forefront of his troops when they ran into devastating fire. His body was never located.

Meanwhile, about three miles east of the Seminary and Cemetery ridges, a clash between Stuart and Union cavalry took place just west of the Low Dutch Road and north of the Hanover Road. Stuart had four brigades (Hampton, Fitzhugh Lee, Jenkins, and Chambles) and Gregg had three (McIntosh, Col. Irvin Gregg, and Custer). Stuart was to go north, then east, and then swing south to hit the Union Army's rear. Now they had been spotted and held fast to a low ridge. Across a small valley was another low ridge just east of Low Dutch Road, where they saw Union troops.

Initially Gregg had only two brigades under his command (McIntosh and Gregg), but as the movement toward battle became obvious, he asked Gen. George Armstrong Custer if he too would help. Custer had been detached from Kilpatrick's division and was now heading back to Big Round Top after completing his reconnaissance mission, but he decided to postpone his return. Always anxious for battle and glory, Custer agreed to help Gregg.

Stuart's men were positioned, dismounted, on Cress Ridge near the Rummel Farm and north of the Hanover Road when the Union signalmen on a ridge just east of Low Dutch Road spotted them. Two Union batteries opened fire, and their fire was returned by Confederate horse

David McM. Gregg's troopers ran into Stuart on the Low Dutch Road and thwarted Lee's plan for a diversion in the Union rear while Pickett assailed the Union line on Cemetery Ridge.

CAVALRY ACTIONS AT GETTYSBURG, 3 JULY 1863

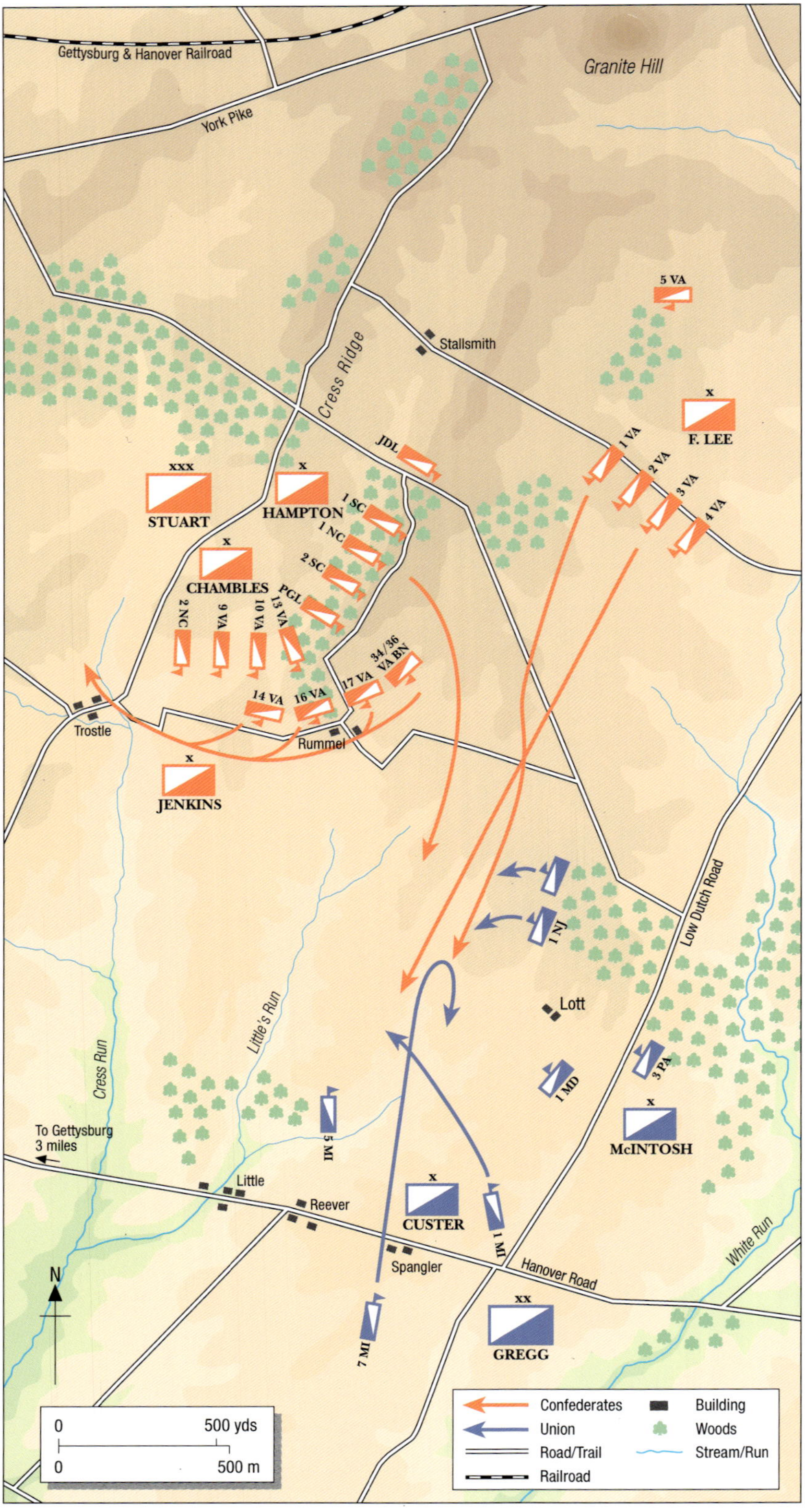

Gettysburg & Hanover Railroad
Granite Hill
York Pike
5 VA
Stallsmith
Cress Ridge
F. LEE
JDL
1 VA
2 VA
3 VA
4 VA
STUART
HAMPTON
1 SC
1 NC
2 SC
CHAMBLES
PGL
2 NC
9 VA
10 VA
13 VA
34/36 VA BN
17 VA
16 VA
14 VA
Trostle
Rummel
JENKINS
1 NJ
Low Dutch Road
Lott
Little's Run
Cress Run
1 MD
3 PA
McINTOSH
5 MI
To Gettysburg 3 miles
Little
Reever
CUSTER
1 MI
Spangler
Hanover Road
White Run
GREGG
7 MI
N
0 500 yds
0 500 m
Confederates
Union
Road/Trail
Railroad
Building
Woods
Stream/Run

J.E.B. Stuart was the epitome of Southern gentility – the last cavalier. He exemplified a code of honor to which others only aspired, and he was arguably the best cavalry commander the South possessed.

Brigadier-general Elon J. Farnsworth's 1st Brigade charged Confederate infantry, cutting through them like a scythe. However, when his brigade re-formed and charged back to Union lines, Farnsworth became one of 60 Union fatalities.

artillery. Near the Rummel farmhouse dismounted skirmishers from Jenkins' and McIntosh's units engaged. For Jenkins' Confederate troops, ammunition was in short supply (they only had ten rounds per man), and the Union artillery and small arms fire from McIntosh's men was getting the better of them. Jenkins had to withdraw. Stuart knew he had to act quickly, and decided a cavalry charge might carry the day and allow him to ride through the Union horsemen and continue his mission. Around 1500 hours Confederate cavalrymen under Wade Hampton and Fitzhugh Lee were mounted and ready to charge. Hampton's and Lee's brigades formed close columns of squadrons with sabers drawn. They advanced under heavy Union artillery and rifle fire, which tore holes in their lines, but still the battle-hardened Southern cavalry continued.

Custer's brigade, mounted and formed in close columns, was ready to meet the Southern charge. His Michigan cavalry rode forward to stop Lee and Hampton's advance.

First Confederate horses broke into a canter, and the Union cavalry followed suit. Then the Confederates galloped, and so did the Union, two mounted units charging at full speed toward each other, sabers drawn and glistening in the afternoon sun. The units collided head-on with a resounding clash that toppled many horses and riders head over heels. In the ensuing mounted mêlée overall organization vanished and small units charged and counter-charged while others tried to regroup and form effective units. In many ways it resembled a brawl more than a military action. Gregg sent his other mounted columns in for flank attacks on the Confederates. Confederate cavalry hero Wade Hampton received a severe saber

This wounded Zouave, possibly a member of the 14th New York, was one of many Zouaves who fought in the Army of the Potomac at Gettysburg.

Although the battle at Lott's Farm began with skirmishing between Chambles' men and Union cavalry, soon Chambles was low on ammunition and his men had to retire.

Almost as daring and dashing as Stuart, and a good commander, Wade Hampton led his cavalry in a charge against Custer in which he received a saber wound that almost cost him his life.

slash to his shoulder. This Union readiness unsettled the Confederates somewhat: they had expected the Union cavalry to break and run. However, the bluecoat troopers had learned something at Brandy Station and in the following days, and sat ahorse knee to knee with the enemy giving as good as they got.

Gradually the cavalry action slowed. The Southerners retired to their original position on Cress Ridge, while disorganized Federal troops remained in the field west of Low Dutch Road. It was 1800 hours.

After darkness fell, and both sides realized that the other was not going to press the battle further, Stuart withdrew to rejoin Lee's command and Custer resumed his trek south to rejoin Pleasonton. Although they did not know it, the battle of Gettysburg was over, and with it ended the realistic hopes for a Confederate military victory or European intervention.

DAY FOUR: 4TH OF JULY

THE COST OF GETTYSBURG

Late on the night of 3 July one of Lee's visitors, Gen. Imboden, noted that Lee lamented that the day past had been "a sad, sad day for us." Later that night he is quoted as saying, "Too bad. Too bad. Oh, too bad." Ironically, the day following the battle for Gettysburg was Independence Day, which commemorated the Declaration of Independence.

Although losses were similar in number, the relative cost to the South was greater because in this battle of attrition, they could not afford to lose the same number of men the Union could. Confederate losses were 4,637 killed, 12,391 wounded, and 5,846 missing or captured. Union losses were 3,149 killed, 14,503 wounded, and 5,161 missing or wounded.

The only Confederate division suffering more than 50% losses was Pickett's, but Confederate brigades with losses greater than 50% included those of Iverson, Garnett, Armistead, Lang, Archer, Pettigrew,

After the battle, these tattered, yet unbowed Confederates surveyed the aftermath of the battlefield at Gettysburg and possibly enjoyed the quiet after the previous three days of carnage.

Photograph of roads leading south from Gettysburg. Instead of Union barriers, Lee encountered only miserable weather, which allowed him to outdistance Meade until he came to the flooded Williamsport crossing.

and Scales. Union divisions with more than 50% losses were Robinson, Wadsworth, and Barlow. Union brigades with losses greater than 50% were those of Stone, Rowley, Paul, Meredith, Ames and Harrow.

Whereas the Union could rebuild their army through increased conscription, because of diminished manpower resources, the Confederates would never be able to fully rebuild their decimated units. Lee's task was now to preserve the Army of Northern Virginia at all costs, because men and materiel lost could not be replaced.

Lee's retreat

On Saturday morning, 4 July, it rained. The gentle and cooling rain brought a mood of peace and serenity to the battlefield where so many Americans had died. Lee realized that with his failure to crush the Army of the Potomac came the spectre of failure for the Confederacy and more trying times for his beloved state of Virginia. He sent a messenger to Gen. Meade suggesting an exchange of prisoners, but Meade did not wish to do so, perhaps feeling that Confederates who were prisoners could not fight against the Union, and after the past three days, he did not wish to face these men again in combat. A stupor seemed to have settled over both armies, but Lee realized that this numbness would not last forever, and so he planned to withdraw that day, before the Union Army could react.

Lee's belief that the Union Army would not attack on the 4th proved correct. Lee planned to withdraw west of the mountains. In fact, it was 48 hours after the battle before the Federals began a somewhat tardy pursuit of the retreating Confederates. As if to mimic Lee's feelings, the rain became a downpour throughout the day while he completed plans for the orderly evacuation of the Army of Northern Virginia. The men heard their marching orders that afternoon. If terrain had benefited the Union, weather aided the Confederacy.

Lee's plan called for evacuation down the Fairfield-Hagerstown Road to Cashtown, west through the Cashtown Gap in the mountains and down into the Cumberland Valley. From there the Army of Northern Virginia would move south to Greenwood, on to Hagerstown, and then

THE CONFEDERATE RETREAT, 4–14 JULY, 1863

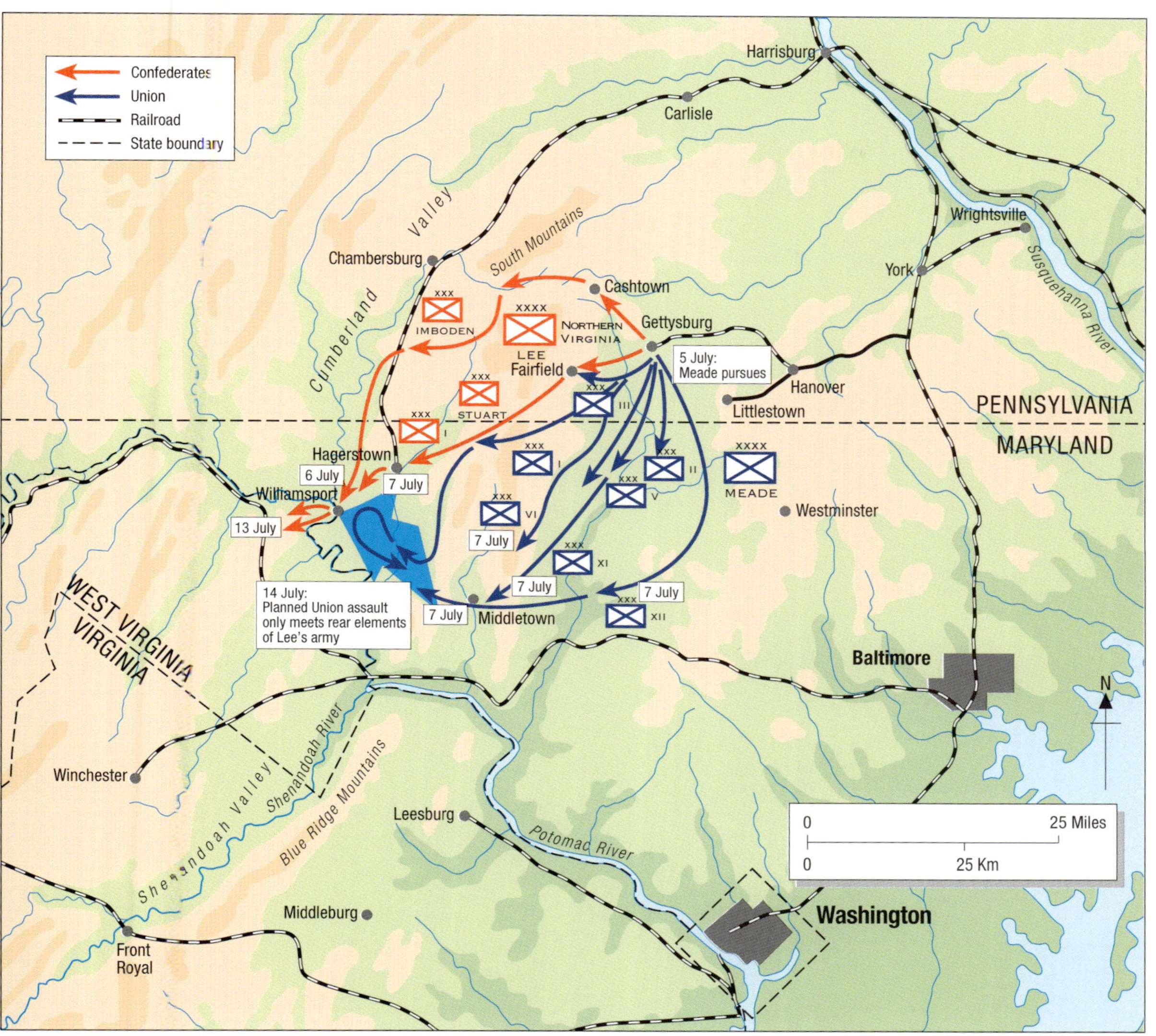

to Williamsport, a distance of a little over 40 miles. Stuart's cavalry was to provide reconnaissance and to hold Cashtown Gap against any Union advance so the slow-moving wagon train could get through without harassment from Union cavalry. Remaining cavalry units would either go south on the Emmitsburg Road to protect the flank or would work with Ewell's Corps to protect the rear. Speed and silence were the essence of his plan, and poor weather his staunch ally.

In the midst of slashing thunderstorms, the Army of Northern Virginia began leaving, the heavy rain and thunder muffling the sounds of their withdrawal. The Hagerstown–Fairfield Road was choked, the wounded escorted by Imboden's command in a column of wagons, ambulances, and ambulatory patients 17 miles long, and then came the infantry. After nightfall Hill evacuated, then Longstreet, and finally Ewell. Stuart's cavalry acted as rearguard and flank escorts for Ewell.

Behind at Gettysburg, the tally of the dead and wounded was

immense, almost a quarter of the total manpower which met there was dead or wounded. Those too badly injured to move, or too close to Union lines to be recovered, were left for the Union Army to care for. Lee's primary concern was harsh – save as much of the Army of Northern Virginia as he could so it would remain a viable threat to both the Army of the Potomac and Washington, D.C. Lee was unhappy with the decision he had to make, but if he was to protect Virginia, he would do whatever necessary, no matter how personally odious.

Rain fell all night long, and well into Sunday. The roads were syrupy mud, slowing wagons and the foot soldiers who slogged along in sodden discomfort. Still, no one tarried, for every Southerner knew that they must put as much distance as possible between themselves and the stationary Union Army.

Cavalry commanders Custer (left) and Pleasonton (right) relax together. Although of lower rank, Custer designed his own flamboyant uniforms, while Pleasonton wore regulation ones.

General W.H. French moved quickly at Meade's orders and reached Williamsport well ahead of Lee. Once there, he destroyed bridges across the flooded Potomac to trap Lee between the pursuing Army of the Potomac and the river itself.

It was nearly noon on 5 July before Meade convinced himself that Lee was really retreating and had not simply withdrawn to regroup for another attack. He ordered Irvin Gregg's cavalry down the Chambersburg Pike to harry the rear elements of Lee's army while Sedgewick's VI Corps infantry moved down the Fairfield Road with much of the Army of the Potomac following. Meade sent orders to French, who had been in reserve at Frederick, to proceed to Williamsport. Once there, French was to destroy the pontoon bridges across the Potomac and to otherwise harass, delay, and destroy the Confederates' route of march and any Southern forces he might encounter.

Meade caught up with the Army of Northern Virginia at Monterey Pass. At first he decided to attack, but after studying the matter he decided that he would dislodge the retreating Southerners from the naturally fortified pass only with the greatest of difficulty and at a high cost. Leaving McIntosh's cavalry and one of Sedgewick's brigades to hold the pass so the Confederates wouldn't attack the rear of his army, Meade followed a route parallel to the Confederate retreat on the eastern side of the mountains. Meade could afford to take his time, for he knew what Lee did not: French was en route to Williamsport to destroy the bridges, and when Lee arrived, he would find himself trapped between the river and the oncoming Union Army.

Kilpatrick's and Buford's cavalry shadowed and constantly sniped at Imboden's columns, but could not bring on a general engagement because of the close proximity of Confederate infantry which all too willingly supported the Southern cavalry. The Union cavalry had to be content with harrying the retreating Confederates.

However, Huey's cavalry brigade of Gregg's division did manage to position itself between the wagon train and Ewell's rearguard during an especially heavy part of the thunderstorm. Rain was so heavy and visibility so poor that they slipped past Ewell without being seen. Lit only by flashes of lightning, the Union cavalry found its way to the top of a steep road descending into the valley near Leiterburg. Just after 0300 hours the Union cavalry came charging out of the heavy night rain into the rear of the wagon train and struck the weary Confederates. Many drivers were wounded or killed; others abandoned their wagons to save themselves. In the midst of the shouting, carbine fire, and peals of thunder, many mules and horses bolted, going over the side of the winding road into the steep ravine or slamming into other wagons and breaking wheels. Finally the Confederates drove off their attackers but many more Southern wounded were now added to the diminished amount of transport available, further slowing Lee's withdrawal.

ABOVE **Imboden was a trusted family friend of Lee's and he was charged with safely returning the wounded and injured to Southern soil. The Confederate cavalry screen was good, but on one occasion, Union cavalry did sneak through to wreak havoc.**

LEFT **Because almost one in five men at Gettysburg died, the task of burying the dead was enormous. Most of the corpses were not buried until after the battle was over, and because of the vast amount of bodies, many were buried in communal graves.**

"The result of this brilliant maneuvre," a Union officer noted, "was the capture of a large number of wagons, ambulances, and mules, with fifteen hundred prisoners." Kilpatrick reported to Meade that Ewell's supplies had been almost totally destroyed, with only five Union men killed, ten wounded, and 28 missing.

French reached Williamsport before the Army of Northern Virginia and destroyed the pontoon bridges, so when Longstreet arrived on 7 July he found his escape path blocked by the raging flood waters. Commandeering boats, he acted quickly and began to ferry men across to the Virginia side, but this task would take two days of constant ferrying without interruption to get only his men across. Getting effectives across, not to mention the wounded, would take at least six. With the close Union pursuit, Lee would either have to make a stand on the northern bank, or sacrifice men in a rearguard action to save the remaining troops in the Army of Northern Virginia.

The Potomac, whose banks were swollen with floodwater from the rains, was an impassable barrier without bridges. After reporting this to Lee, Longstreet and Lee immediately threw up defences from Downsville around to Falling Waters on Concoteague Creek, both ends of the five-mile line secured by water. At Gettysburg, he may have been on the offensive, but here Longstreet was in his element, and with Lee's approval, he began throwing up fortifications. If Meade attacked, he would pay dearly. Meade pushed his army south, and by 9 July he could see the Confederate positions. However, all his army was not present, and he would need every man he had if the Army of the Potomac was to win this battle. Meade sent a message to Halleck telling him where he was and that he intended to attack Lee once the full Union Army materialized. By 12 July Meade's army was in place. He discussed the situation with his commanders prior to an attack. His commanders were uncertain as to how many Confederates they faced: five of his seven corps commanders disagreed with his plan to attack the Southerners. The following day, 13 July, 1863 Meade personally surveyed the Confederate defenses to gauge how strong they were and how many men he faced. A concentrated Union push would force the Confederates to fight or flee. Either way, he would devastate them. He ordered his men to attack the following morning.

The Confederates knew a Union attack was imminent. On 13 July warehouses in the town were torn down and Confederates fashioned a makeshift pontoon bridge from the foraged lumber. Observers called it a patchwork bridge, and although Lee pronounced it fit, many men started across hesitantly, staring down into the still turbulent (but receding) waters uncertainly as they made their way across. Ewell's men were fording the river upstream since the waters had subsided sufficiently for them to wade chest-high across to the Virginia shore.

Longstreet crossed safely into Virginia. At 0300 hours on 14 July Federal cavalry noted that Confederates were leaving their positions and withdrawing across the river into Virginia. Meade ordered the attack to commence earlier than originally planned, hoping to stop the Confederate withdrawal. A.P. Hill's Corps was the last to withdraw. Most of them made it across the bridge before cavalry under Buford and Kilpatrick attacked their rear units – Heth's division. When he heard the sounds of battle, Lee's appeared resigned: "There. I was expecting it. The beginning of the attack!"

ABOVE **The ambulance in the background was used as a makeshift hearse. This is the same sort of vehicle Lee's wounded were placed in during the retreat which began during a thunderstorm the day after the battle of Gettysburg.**

RIGHT **A period lithograph showing the Union cavalry belatedly pursuing Lee's Army of Northern Virginia on July 12th, crossing the bridge at Antietam near the scene of a pyrrhic victory a year earlier.**

Pettigrew's men were first to fight at Gettysburg, and the last ones to cross the makeshift bridge back into Virginia. During that final battle, Pettigrew was mortally wounded.

Custer's 6th Michigan charged Heth's men, and the Confederates turned to fight. Onrushing Yankee cavalry rode into determined Confederate volleys. In four minutes the 6th Michigan was dissipated by small arms fire, and the Southern withdrawal continued a pace. Pettigrew brought up the rear. Still, the charge of the 6th Michigan had bought the Union valuable time by slowing the Confederate retreat and allowing them to bring forward reinforcements. Another Union attack slammed into the Confederate rearguard. This time, it was successful, capturing almost 1,500 Confederates, and when it was over, Gen. Pettigrew lay dying. The sacrifice of Heth's Confederates allowed the last units to make it safely to Virginia, and after the last of them had cleared the bridge, they cut the pontoons loose from their moorings as Buford's cavalry thundered down to the bridge site. As the battle of Gettysburg had begun, with Heth and Pettigrew, so it ended.

Lincoln was desolated by the escape of the Army of Northern Virginia, knowing that the South was far from crushed and would still be able to fight. "We had them within our grasp," he said to his secretary, "...all we had to do was stretch forth our hands..."

The Confederate Army survived to fight another 20 months, but with Grant's victory at Vicksburg and Meade's at Gettysburg, hopes of a Southern victory faded, until Petersburg and Appomattox extinguished them.

GETTYSBURG TODAY

Today Gettysburg is a quiet town. Located an hour and a half from Washington, D.C., this battlefield draws visitors from all over the world. Gettysburg National Military Park is open year-round. Although parts are commercialized, the attractions are low-key and an aura of reverence pervades the site of the American Civil War's pivotal battle.

The town of Gettysburg lies four minutes off Interstate I-70, and tourists driving to the battlefield exit onto State Road 15, which happens to be the Emmitsburg Road. Driving due north, they pass the battlefield park whose main parking lot and visitor center are situated to the right (east) side of (State Road) SR 15 approximately one half-mile before the downtown area. The visitor center is north of Bloody Angle, at the northern end of Cemetery Ridge, and has a parking lot.

Gettysburg National Military Park occupies both sides of SR 15. Free parking is available at the visitor center, Oak Hill, Little Round Top, the artillery park and other areas. The United States Park Service has an excellent museum at Gettysburg, which incorporates an extensive armory (free) and many uniforms on display (free) as well as a lighted map program (nominal charge) showing the progression of the battle and an audio-visual presentation. There are guided tours and audio tours. For those who do not wish to hike over the rather large battlefield from Oak Hill south to Big Round Top and from Culp's Hill west over to Herr's Ridge, the auto tour's route is clearly marked. Visitors to the park can drive to within 100 feet of most sites, park, and then walk to the area. The battlefield park covers 28 kilometers (18 miles) and all is accessible by automobile. This is especially important to international visitors who may not be prepared for the summer temperatures of 90 degrees or more and high humidity which sap strength and deplete initiative.

Licensed guides are available for the battlefield auto tours, but call in advance for information to make sure a guide will be available. For youth groups attending mid-April through mid-October, on-battlefield camp sites are available. Contact the Park Service at Gettysburg National Military Park, Gettysburg, PA 17325, for full details, and be sure to include the days and time of the group's visit.

Of particular interest is a ten-minute video loop shown on the downstairs level of the visitor's center depicting an actual Civil War vintage cannon being fired by Civil War re-enactors and showing how members of the gun crew serve the piece. In the same building is a book and gift shop which contains many volumes on not only Gettysburg but also other Civil War sites and units. At the front desk, the information booth has free tour maps of the site and the receptionists are willing to help visitors locate specific areas they wish to see and give instructions on which route to take to reach them. Just south (about half a block) of the visitor center is the Cyclorama, which includes a film (free) and the famous painting of Pickett's Charge by Paul Philipoteaux, depicting all the events in Pickett's Charge. It is accompanied by a sound and light program.

The park has four trails the visitor can walk: the High Water Mark Trail, the Big Round Top Loop Trail, the Billy Yank Trail, and the Johnny Reb Trail. In addition, there are paths to the Devil's Den, Point of Woods, and a self-guided tour through the National Cemetery. The High Water Tour is a mile long and covers the Cyclorama, Meade's headquarters and the Union defence of the Bloody Angle. The Big Round Top Loop covers wildlife, animals, and is about three and a half miles long. The Billy Yank is nine miles long and the Johnny Reb is three and a half miles. The latter two are part of the Boy Scouts of America's Heritage Walk.

Southwest of the park is the home of President (Gen.) Dwight D. Eisenhower, and on the battlefield near the Bloody Angle is a tree which commemorates the post-Civil War army camp where the idea for the United States Army's armour branch was born. This is located on the east side of SR 15, about 20 feet off the road and on the western slope of the ridge below the Cyclorama.

The battlefield can easily be toured within a day, but there is a great deal to take in, so allow yourself ample time to visit and take photographs. Also, spend some time in the town of Gettysburg, which has many historic buildings, shops, and landmarks.

Just north and slightly east of the visitor's center lies the National Cemetery, where many of the soldiers who died here, in what has been called the second Revolutionary War of the United States, are buried.

WARGAMING GETTYSBURG

Gettysburg is not an easy battle to game, but is perhaps the most gamed American Civil War battle when one considers the amount of military strategy, popular board games, or miniatures scenarios available. Scarcely a gaming convention goes by without one or more portions of the battle being refought. At a recent convention, with scarcely 120 attendees, eight unrelated events were parts of Gettysburg.

Why is it so popular? For one thing, most Americans probably had a great-great grandfather or two at Gettysburg. More importantly, this battle could have gone either way, and it offers tactical and grand strategical opportunities because the ebb and flow of battle do not make it a cut and dried set piece. Lee won the first day; the second day was inconclusive; and the Union clearly won on the third day, yet they did not so much crush as allow their enemy to smash themselves against the Union Army's defensive line and wear themselves to a halt through the bloodiest attrition in any day of fighting in the Civil War.

At the time, neither side was satisfied that Gettysburg had been a conclusive battle. It is only in the cold light reflected from 130 years and more of history that we see the battle as the turning point of the war.

Gaming the entire battle is either a test of endurance or intellect, because with standard miniature rules, most games that try to be comprehensive recreations of the battle run for multiple days, certainly much longer than the actual battle itself. The best way to game Gettysburg is to break it up into bite-sized pieces and then game them one at a time, whether pushing counters around on a map or moving Minifigs across Woodland Scenics Wheat Fields.

Nowhere is it more clear to the novice what the term 'fog of war' means, especially when one considers the effect of Stuart's absence on Confederate military intelligence. Lee not only did not know whom he faced (he didn't immediately realize Meade had replaced Hooker), but the Union Army credited the Confederacy with having more troops present at the battle than they actually had. Having all the facts at hand today, it is easy to dissect an engagement and say who should have done what, but when one considers the uncertainty of combat with limited intelligence, one begins to appreciate the real scope and breadth of Gettysburg.

Time was as much against them as was the enemy. If Heth had been more aggressive and his brigades better led, Meade wouldn't have been able to send Reynolds to reinforce the town and the battle would have been fought 12 miles south of Gettysburg to the Union's great disadvantage terrain-wise.

The best skirmish actions are either an encounter on July 1st between elements of Heth's Division and the 8th Illinois of Buford's command (a classic meeting of dismounted cavalry fighting a delaying action against a superior amount of infantry with just the tiniest bit of artillery available off-board), or the cavalry skirmish between J.E.B. Stuart and McIntosh on 3 July (skirmishers on both sides escalating the fray into a cavalry versus cavalry slugfest). Both actions are manageable and involve relatively few pieces.

For those who wish a rough and tumble engagement, try gaming Chamberlain against Oates on Little Round Top. There are no cavalry, and just a few artillery pieces nearby, but the terrain provides evenly matched cover, and neither side has too many troops. With a timetable and some random die rolls to see which troops are available and at what times, this can be engrossing.

The battle for the Wheat Field and Devil's Den give gamers the opportunity to move masses of troops, receive reinforcements, plan some strategy and still become involved in mass mêlée without cavalry involvement and only minimal artillery support. Near Emmitsburg Road, both sides have opportunities to advance, charge, and retreat as reinforcements upset the balance.

The most played game is Pickett's Charge. Just as Napoleonic gamers crave to test their wits and luck with Waterloo, so Civil War gamers want to see if they can make it across the road and break the Union line. Of course, Pickett's Charge is uneven and provides the Union player with an advantage of a fortified defensive position, but the Confederate player does get to move a lot of troops back and forth across the gaming area. However, it requires only minimal scenery: a copse of trees, some low walls, and a field which slopes slightly upward at its eastern end.

The ultimate game, however, is fighting the Confederate withdrawal to the river, over the rainy and fog-swept mountains, to the town where Confederates could retreat into the safe haven of Virginia. The game here is not how the armies can clash mightily, but who can out-think and outmaneuvre his opponent.

There are many rules sets and, of course, either 15mm or 25mm figures can be used, but for skirmish gaming, 25mm seem best, while 15mm are well suited to Pickett's Charge. For those gamers who have great eyesight, 6mm troops would give a grand scope of the charge which could be gamed on the dining room table between meals.

For those desiring to set up a miniatures game, read one of Pfanz's books about the second day, and then follow up with Wheeler's book to get the feel of the conflict blow by blow and also get the impressions of individual actions by those present at Gettysburg. Plan carefully, and approach this as not just a game to be experienced and then forgotten, but as a test of intellect and luck which can be gamed over and over with players alternating commands of the Union or Confederate forces. It becomes almost an abstract strategy simulation similar to chess, because Gettysburg challenges all lovers of history.

INDEX

(References to illustrations are shown in **bold**.)